ADVANCE PRAISE FOR THE GARAGE BAND METHOD

"The Garage Band Method is a step-by-step approach to making real music with real people and having real fun."

– Gregory Yasinitsky, Director of Jazz Studies, Washington State University

"This method is great for establishing your ability to play with other musicians, which is what makes music come to life."

– Ken Morton, owner, Musicians' Pro Shop, Boise, Idaho

"This is a darned intelligent system."

– Dan Gunnerson, university student and former salesman, Musicians' Pro Shop, Boise Idaho (who swiped his boss's proof and read it one slow afternoon.)

"This is a brilliant approach. Anybody who can read can understand what's going on here."

– Andy A., bassist, 8 Ball Break

"This book needed to be written."

– Ken Harris, co-owner, The Blues Bouquet, Boise, Idaho

The Garage Band Method

— How the Rest of Us Can Learn to Play —

If you want to help someone,

teach them a song.

~ Hungarian Proverb

THE GARAGE BAND METHOD

How the *rest* of us can learn to play . . .

Really play

By Bill Hargrove and Bob Ratcliff

Artwork, design and typography by Christine Latter

Camel's Back Press

The Garage Band Method: How the Rest of Us Can Learn to Play ... Really Play

For information, contact Camel's Back Press, 1156 Santa Maria Drive, Boise, Idaho 83712.
ISBN 1-889975-00-1

My part of this work is dedicated to my mom, my dad and Dexter Gordon.

~ Bob Ratcliff

My part of this work is dedicated to all the people who have brought music into my life, most notably my father-in-law, Ed Brunner, and my co-author, Bob.

~ Bill Hargrove

Table of Contents

THE BEST LEARNING METHOD FOR YOU

There is no "best" way to teach everybody. In most disciplines, however, there is a best way to teach particular individuals. That's because people have different learning styles.

That's one reason our schools, including our music programs, do such a good job of teaching some people, but not others. A school generally does well with people who have learning styles that jibe with the way the school teaches, and not so well with those whose learning styles don't fit.

So ... this book does not purport to be the "best" approach to learning music. Rather, it is meant to open the world of playing music to a new segment of the population, i.e., people whose learning styles don't mesh with traditional ways of teaching music.

We've aimed this book at people with learning styles that have the following characteristics:

- A desire to read about and understand a task before trying it.
- A desire to learn intuitively, by doing, rather than through rote memorization.
- A willingness and ability to look at a task from a different perspective.
- The ability to work with other people.
- The ability to squelch the fear of looking silly.

HOW TO USE THIS BOOK

If you follow the instructions in this book you will, in a surprisingly short time, be able to play rock 'n' roll, blues, country or similar music with a lot of good bands. You'll be able to play at jam sessions and even sit in with terrific players who like to encourage beginners. The best way to go about it is to:

- **Read the book all the way through. If you do, you will understand how most music is made, which will double the likelihood that you'll learn to play, even if you don't choose to follow our instructions to the letter.**
- Find the kind of teacher described in the chapter entitled *How to Find the Right Teacher*. (Or find substitutes, as described in the chapter on teaching yourself.)
- Have the teacher (or substitutes) lead you through the course of study described in the book.
- Practice at least 20 minutes every day.
- Start a garage band.

Preface

THE PLAN

We wrote this book with the hope of abetting a long-term campaign to infiltrate every American neighborhood, town and city with new musicians — young, old, middle-aged, women, men, hip, square and otherwise. Our country can easily have three or four times as many people playing music as it does now — if those of us who play can only make other people understand how to go about it.

When approached in the right way, playing music is no more difficult than softball, golf, tennis, bowling, mountain biking, fly fishing, yoga, sewing, karate, woodworking, tai chi, aikido or basketball. If we can just help people understand that, we can have many, many more people jamming at home with friends.

That's our dream – a world in which you can walk through your neighborhood on a summer night and hear the sounds of people playing music.

Think of hearing a piano and saxophone playing the sweet strains of *Ain't Misbehavin'* through an open window on your street. Or electric guitar rock well-muffled behind a garage door somewhere in the neighborhood. Or kids on a street corner singing four-part doo-wop harmony. Or a hunk in a cowboy hat picking a country tune on a park bench. Or two old women on a front porch knocking down blues on harmonica and acoustic guitar. Or a flute and violin playing Mozart in somebody's back yard. Imagine looking through a casement window into a basement apartment to see and hear weird-looking college kids swirling through an incomprehensible bebop jazz tune. Imagine aunts, uncles, cousins, brothers, sisters, etc. hanging around a piano after Sunday dinner, singing.

That's the kind of world in which everyone ought to live. We hope this book will help make it happen.

A HOLISTIC APPROACH

We believe that millions of people would like to play music and could, but don't because they don't understand how music is made or the modest personal requirements for making it. That's why we wrote this book – to explain.

This method is not like any approach to music you've ever read about, but is almost exactly the same as the way a child learns its native language. The child first learns to communicate in simple ways and then builds on that success every day. It works for music just as it does for language, because music is a language, too.

Seven things make the method work:

• An understanding that the easiest way to start playing music is by "grooving" along with other musicians or a recording, getting into the rhythm with whatever primitive skills you possess, whether it's tapping out time or playing two-note riffs on a sax.

Chris, the artist who designed this book,called me at 8:15 one morning. "You're going to love this," she said. "I took my draft of the book home last night, just to see if it really works." She had tried our approach on an old guitar that had been hanging around their house for years. "You were right," she said. "It took me about 20 minutes to get going. I was so excited I went upstairs and woke up Fred."

Chris Latter

• A personal introduction to one form of simple, but elegant, music – the 12-bar blues – which can be used as a tool to learn to play any music. As soon as you understand this blues form and can coax a six-note blues scale from whatever instrument you choose, you can play along by ear with any recording of a 12-bar blues in the key of that scale. You can do it with special play-along tapes and CDs like we sell, or you can do it with the hundreds of 12-bar-blues tunes that have been recorded by blues, rock, country and jazz artists from Elvis to B.B. King to K.D. Lang. As you master the blues, you can then move on to more complex music.

• An observation borrowed from the Whole Language movement in reading: Learning is easy and enjoyable if the material is useful to you right now.

• Learning how music works.

• An understanding that most of the music Americans enjoy – rock, pop, blues, country, etc. – is extremely simple.

• Understanding that even if you think you're tone deaf, you have an innate ability to make music by ear, i.e. by listening, then singing along, whistling or making tones on a musical instrument. (Moreover, you can learn to "hear" music better through ear training, formally or informally, just by listening to and playing music.)

• Persuading yourself to track down people with musical skills similar to your own – no matter how crude – and making music with them as soon as possible.

THE GARAGE BAND METHOD

1

IF YOU WANT TO PLAY MUSIC

We designed this book to help you understand how anyone can learn to play music in a reasonable amount of time with a reasonable amount of effort. And we mean really play – with confidence and flair. The secret is understanding the most intuitive way to develop a command of any musical instrument – much the same way that people have been learning to play blues guitar for a hundred years.

It's no accident that a lot more people play guitar than any other instrument. The main reason is that the traditional way of learning to play guitar is by improvising over simple popular music, which works great, whereas the traditional way of learning other instruments is by reading music, starting with children's songs, which too often leads to frustration, boredom and failure.

Generations of rock, blues and country guitar players have learned by methods simi-

A Note to Readers Who Play or Played

If you took piano lessons or played in school band as a kid, then this book is as much or more for you as for the novice. Our approach is nothing like what you did when you read music in band or at piano lessons. We free you from the written page and show you how to make music by improvising, the way most professional musicians do it. Your past experience will give you a big advantage, however. Even if you haven't played for a long time, you still possess lots of technique and musical knowledge that will help you progress quickly.

lar to the one we describe. They all did pretty much the same thing. They got themselves an instrument of some sort. They got somebody to show them how to lay down a simple groove. And they practiced that simple groove along with a recording or a more accomplished parent, sibling, aunt, uncle or friend. When they started getting the hang of it, they rounded up several amigos of similar ambition and formed a garage (or back porch or living room) band. From then on, they made music together and gradually got better.

A Note to Quibblers

We're likely to get into trouble with some blues guitarists who'll adamantly maintain that they didn't learn to play by improvising. We won't argue that point, because that point depends on how you define improvise. We will, however, go to the mat to defend our proposition that most successful blues guitarists learn simple grooves very early in their careers, start having fun with those simple grooves early on, then grow from there. Whether you call that improvising or copying the licks of your idol is just semantics. The learning process is the same. The only difference is where you find the tools for grooving.

The concept is simple. You learn an easy way to groove along with recordings or live musicians by playing just a few good notes. Then, as you play and have fun, you gradually obtain a basic command of your instrument and music of all kinds. Two things make it work – the fun and maximizing the fun by playing with other people as soon as possible. Practice is what makes musicians, and fun is what inspires you to practice.

Think of Music as a Sport

To understand this learning process, it helps to look at music as a sport. In most sports, you use the big muscles in your arms and legs, guiding them with your eyes. In music, you use smaller muscles and guide them with your ears. When you learned to play baseball as a little kid, you didn't go to a class and study how to swing a bat or throw a ball. You went out in the yard and played with your friends. You did your best each day and gradually got better, training your muscles as you played and received pointers from people who already knew how to play baseball.

That's exactly the way you can learn to make music, playing with a small group of friends. A pick-up jam session for rank novice musicians can be just as much fun as a pick-up baseball game for rank novice little kids. You will also improve just as fast as those little kids.

This book tells you how to get started, equip yourself and gather people together for such jam sessions. (For a closer look at the musician as athlete, see neurologist Frank Wilson's 1986 book, *Tone Deaf & All Thumbs?*)

You Must Play With Other People

We don't know how to say this except to say it. If you will start playing music with a small group of friends as soon as possible, you will almost certainly succeed at becoming a musician. On the other hand, if you don't start playing music with people near the beginning of this endeavor, you probably will not succeed.

The Method Works

I know this method works because it worked for me. I was 42 when I started taking tenor sax lessons from Bob Ratcliff, who now is my co-author. At the start, I could barely make a saxophone honk. Within six months, I was playing in a blues band with two guitar players, a bassist, a drummer and a singer-harmonica player. Within another six months, our band was playing free gigs. Within another six months, we started playing paid gigs, which we do all the time now. We're not great musicians, but we play great songs, have fun and make music that people enjoy.

We Don't Mean to Replace School Band

When we talk about good teaching methods driving out bad, we're not talking about us putting school bands and orchestras out of business. That's a whole different ball game. We haven't come up with a way to teach improvisation to a band room filled with 30 or 40 kids, which is as much a matter of crowd control as of music. Until we do, we'd like to suggest that learning improvisation through our method is something kids should do in addition to what they learn in the band room.

Start a Garage Band Today

Above all else, this book is about being a participant rather than a spectator. Bob and I have had tons of fun playing music with friends in back bedrooms, garages and living rooms. You can do the same. Musical instruments are for making music today at whatever skill level you happen to possess. You don't have to be Michael Jordan to play basketball in the driveway or Julia Child to cook up a killer burrito. Playing music with friends is similar. Great skill is not the primary ingredient. You don't have to be Eric Clapton or Itzhak Perlman. You just have to do it. When the planets line up, the result **will** be art. That's where we're headed with this book. We want to put everyone with the time and inclination to work playing a musical instrument in a garage band or living room ensemble.

This Isn't Just Us; It's a Movement

To be honest, my partner, Bob, didn't dream the Garage Band method up by himself. We're part of a movement in music. Other people all around the country are providing similar teaching methods and self-help materials. Patty Carlson produced her *Play the Blues Overnight* video, which introduces students to the piano through improvisation. Yesterday[1], I attended a workshop for high school students where jazz trumpeter Wynton Marsalis said many of the same things we say in this book. Gerald Eskelin of the L.A. Jazz Choir has published a book called *Lies My Music Teacher Told Me,* which eloquently explains why students who start out improvising succeed and so many who start out learning to read musical notation don't succeed. PG Music sells *Band in a Box* software, which will turn your computer and stereo into the kind of play-along rhythm section that we recommend you use to make practicing more fun. Jamey Aebersold, who started the movement about 20 years ago, sells thousands of play-along CDs and instructional booklets that are geared to more advanced jazz students but espouse the same principles we espouse. Guitarist Happy Traum sells audio, video and written materials on improvisation through his Homespun Tapes mail order house. Mel Bay, the giant of the guitar instruc-

You Are Not Tone Deaf

The ability to "hear" and then repeat music is not a God-given talent that some have and others don't. It's a learned skill, developed primarily through listening. Obviously, some people have more of a knack for it than others, but very few have ears that lack the physical ability to differentiate tones. The rest of us do. We just have to develop the skill the way you do any other. One way is simply to listen to music. Playing music is a faster way. If you want to speed things up more, you can work through an ear-training course. There are lots of them available on CD. Every music school offers them, too.

[1] April 12, 1995

tion business, is heading the same direction with new videos. There's even a national organization for musical improvisers, Music For People. It has chapters all over the country that bring people together – both novices and the more accomplished – to improvise music.

This movement is coming about naturally because good methods drive out bad ones. Gradually, people are discovering you don't have to begin playing by learning to read music one klutzy note of *Mary Had a Little Lamb* at a time, but can start instead by picking up a few simple licks by ear. When that happens, they don't buy the old klutzy method any more. This book is just another step in the movement, an attempt to systematize, unify and improve upon what people are doing independently all over the country.

2

HOW TUNES AND MUSICIANS WORK

Most people think of a song as the melody and the words, but that perception is misleading. A song is like a person's body. The melody and words are just the exterior. Hiding beneath the exterior is a skeleton that gives the song its basic structure. This skeleton is made up of a series of chords called a progression. The chords, their order and their duration give the song its essence.

Chord: *several notes played together to create a particular sound or emotional feeling.*

The next element that's added to the skeleton of a tune is the rhythm pattern. The chord-playing instruments in the rhythm section (usually bass, rhythm guitar and/or piano) play the chord progression in a specific rhythm pattern to give the tune its shape or feel, e.g. Latin, waltz, rock, country, blues, etc. No matter what the chord

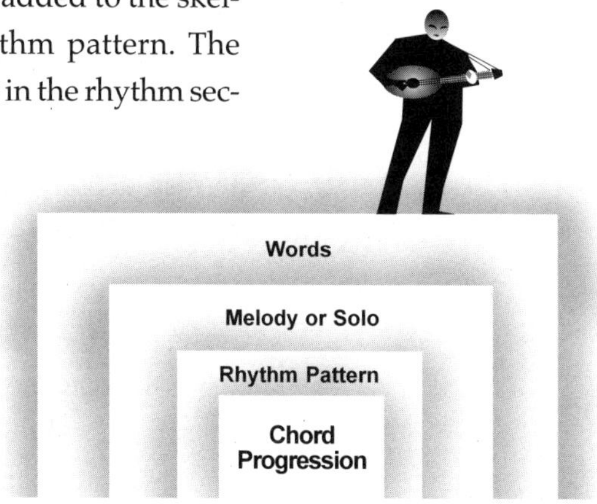

Structure of a Song

progression, if you change the rhythm pattern from swing to Latin, then you change the feel from swing to Latin.

The melody is the final musical layer to be added. It is simply a series of notes that sound good with whatever chord is being played at any given point. The melody by which you identify a song is just one of many that will work with a given chord progression. You can create any number of such melodies because there are bunches of notes that will sound fine with each chord. When a soloist improvises, he or she creates one of these new melodies by stringing together some of these "good" notes.

The last element added to a song is its words. That's the outer layer.

That's a song: you start with a chord progression, you add a rhythm pattern, then you lay the melody and words (or an improvised solo) over the top.

Most Popular Music is Improvised

Almost all popular music such as rock, country and blues is improvised. You can't really play it the way it's supposed to be played by reading notes on a page. Even the people who write songs seldom play them exactly the same way twice. That's why different recordings of the same song often sound a lot different.

What a Musician Does When He or She Improvises

We want you to learn to play music by improvising because it's easier and because that's the way most popular music is played. To understand this approach, it helps to first understand what a musician does as he or she improvises over a blues, country, pop or jazz tune. A majority of the popular music you hear played by professional musicians is improvised. If the song has words, the singers sing the written melody, but the instrumentalists often improvise other parts. If a song doesn't have words, the instrumentalists usually play the melody once at the beginning and once at the end, but improvise the solos in between. This happens in all of the most popular styles of music – rock, blues, country, pop, jazz, reggae, new age, all of it. You can't play this kind of music the way it's supposed to be played by reading notes on a page.

How do you do it, then?

To visualize how professionals play popular music, it is simplest to think about a solo instrument like the saxophone, because the sax has one primary job – to lay a melody line or improvised solo over the top of the chord progression. (Pianists and guitarists, on the other hand, have two jobs. Sometimes they play solos, but most of the time they play rhythm, which will be explained later.)

Here's how an accomplished saxophonist (or pianist or guitarist) creates an improvised solo.

First of all, he or she knows the chord progression of the song, its skeleton. With the chord progression in mind, the accomplished player can mentally hear a "melody" or improvised solo that will fit over the progression. This "pre-hearing" sometimes takes place, full-blown, before the solo starts. More often, the pre-hearing takes place in pieces, meaning the musician "pre-hears" a single phrase or even a single note only as the tune moves from one chord to another. In the latter case, the solo unfolds as the player moves through the tune.

There also can be an added twist to this "unfolding" approach. In some cases, the player won't actually pre-hear the next note or notes. Instead, he will "intellectually" pick notes that his knowledge of chords tells him will sound good with the chord being played at that moment.

The solo emerges as the player plays and hears the notes for the first time. The result may surprise him as much as his listeners.

Scale: *a series of notes that are a specified musical distance apart. The one with which most of us are familiar is the major scale: Do Re Mi Fa So La Ti Do. There are lots of other scales that have different sounds.*

The Knowledge and Skills Needed to Do What We Just Described

A **completely** accomplished musician has a skill that is like the skill you use to sing a song. When you sing, you imagine the melody and you automatically adjust your vocal chords to produce the right notes. You don't have to think about how long or short to make your vocal chords. You can just **do** it because you've practiced doing it all your life. A completely accomplished musician has the same relationship with his or her instrument. The mental ear hears the note to be played and the muscles that control the instrument do whatever they need to do to produce the note.

This ability is, of course, an ideal. Many terrific improvisers can't even come close to doing what we've described. They are not nearly so precise. Instead of playing exactly what they "pre-hear," they approximate it by playing notes they know will at least be in the vicinity of the notes they imagine. Or they may not pre-hear a precise melody at all. Instead, they may simply have a musical sketch in their heads. They fill in the sketch as they move through the tune, playing some notes by ear and others intellectually, picking notes they know will work with a chord even though they're not quite sure how the notes will sound. Most of the musicians you hear in your local clubs fit into this category.

This less-than-perfect player is the one to study, because anyone can do what he or she does. This person starts out playing a tune armed with four things:

- The basic knowledge of the tune's chord progression (or the ability to read chords on a page);
- The ability to play some things from memory – whole melodies or shorter licks (a lick is just a short musical statement, which could be made up of as few as two or three notes, or could run several measures and lots of notes);
- The ability to play some things by ear; and
- The ability to reach out and experiment by playing notes he or she intellectually "knows" will sound all right over a given chord, whether or not he or she can hear them in advance.

When such a player solos, these abilities work together. The player may move from a memorized lick to a lick created by ear in re-

As I write, Brian Murphy is in the eighth grade. When he started taking lessons from Bob at the beginning of the seventh grade, he couldn't get a real tone out of his alto sax. By the end of the seventh grade, he could improvise blues in a half dozen keys, was starting to play jazz, and was learning Charlie Parker's solo on a blues tune called *Bloomido*. A while back, when his mom asked about the value of his lessons, he responded, "Mom, if it wasn't for Bob, I'd suck."

Brian Murphy

sponse to another player, **then** on to an experimental lick made up of intellectually selected "surprise" notes, **then** may react to that creation by playing something else from memory or by ear, etc., etc.

Regular Practice

If you practice 20 minutes or more a day using our method, you will learn to play. More importantly, we're betting that as you learn to play, you'll want to practice more than 20 minutes a day, which is advisable if you want to satisfy the natural human craving for rapid improvement. Our approach is designed to lure you into that practice, by making it fun, but the decision is still up to you. If you don't practice regularly, you almost certainly won't learn to play.

The Hard-to-Define Nature of Some Musical Skills/Knowledge

In music as in other physical endeavors, the line between knowing and doing sometimes gets fuzzy. That's because when we perform physical acts quickly, we don't just know how to do them in our heads, we also "know" how to do them in our muscles. We have muscle memory. When a musician plays a note by ear, his brain doesn't consciously say play such and such a note. The brain simply imagines a note and the muscles play it. Something similar happens when a musician has to make an intellectual choice of notes. His mind will consciously say something like this: "The rhythm section is playing chord X, and I know that any of the notes in scale Y will go with that chord, so I am going to have my muscles play notes from scale Y." At that point, however, the conscious direction will give way to the muscle memory of that scale, which has been played so many times in practice that the muscles can play the notes of the scale without waiting for conscious direction.

How to Acquire this Combination of Knowledge and Muscle Memory

The traditional way to learn this stuff is through memorization and drills. By hard work, you cement the knowledge of written music into your head. Through repetition of scale drills, you lock the memory of scales into your muscles. We prefer to learn by doing – through our own version of on-the-job training. In the Garage Band method, you start out playing simple, but cool, music. You have fun, so you play more. As you move ahead, you painlessly acquire knowledge and muscle memory. As you do that, you gradually increase the sophistication of what you play – under the guidance of a teacher – so you keep acquiring more knowledge and muscle memory. When you reach the point where you need to play scale or chord drills to get better, you want to do it because it helps you improve quickly – which is fun.

12-Bar Blues

Throughout this book we will be talking about 12-bar blues, which is the most common blues form, the standard. It has a standard length – 12 "bars" or "measures" of four beats each. It also has a standard chord progression, which we will discuss later. It is a handy teaching tool for a number of reasons, the most significant of which is that hundreds of familiar blues, rock and country songs are 12-bar blues.

The Steps Along the Way

Our "generic" description of an improvising musician's knowledge and skills applies to a broad range of players, some with highly refined abilities, others whose talents are not so polished. For example, Bob does what we've described over complicated jazz chord progressions, making highly sophisticated choices of notes. I do the same thing over simple blues chord progressions, making some fairly mundane choices of notes. If you put us on a 10 scale, he'd be an eight and I'd be a three, but I still sound darn good. You will start out in the Garage Band method as a one, but will sound pretty good, too.

Here's the difference between being an eight like Bob, a two-and-a-half like me or a one like you'll be:

An Eight Like Bob: Bob is so familiar with all chords, that he can deal with them individually, even when there are 20 in a fast-paced tune. He also has a variety of ways he can choose "good" notes to play with each chord. He knows the notes of the chord itself, so he can play any of them. He knows a half dozen scales whose notes go with the chord, so he can choose from any of them. And he has a sophisticated ear, so he can pick out notes that way, too.

A Two-and-a-Half Like Me: Unlike Bob, I am not familiar with all chords. I am, however, pretty familiar with the simplest family of chords. By pretty familiar, I mean if a tune has only three of these simple chords – as a 12-bar blues does – then I can deal with them pretty effectively using the limited tools at my disposal. I can play chord tones. Or I can play notes from one of the three scales that I know go with those chords. Or I can play by ear, though not nearly as adeptly as Bob. (Most musicians in your local clubs are threes, fours and fives on this scale.)

A One Like You: The Garage Band method will start you out doing exactly what Bob and I do, but in a way that's even simpler than mine. The main way we simplify things is by having you play along with a recorded rhythm section playing a 12-bar blues chord progression. To do that, all you have to learn is two things: 1) how to play the six notes of the blues scale in the key in which you're playing and 2) that any of those six notes will sound "good" with any of the three chords in the 12-bar blues progression being played on the recording. Which means that when you first take a stab at soloing, you will have only one way to do it – by experimentally playing any of the six notes of that blues scale in any way you please, along with the recording. They may sound awkward at first, but your ear soon will begin developing the ability to pick out simple licks using those notes. Within a short time more, you will begin committing those simple licks to memory. And at that point, you will have the rudimentary versions of all the four elements of playing we described above, namely:

- Basic knowledge of the chord progression of the tune to be played. (You'll know it's a 12-bar blues progression, even if you don't know the individual chords. That's enough at the beginning.);
- The ability to play some licks from memory;
- A limited ability to play by ear; and
- The ability to reach out and pick notes from a set you intellectually "know" will sound all right over the chords being played by the rhythm section, i.e, the blues scale in that key.

The rest of learning to play a musical instrument is to expand each of those abilities in a step-by-step manner. What's nice is that the memorization and playing by ear will come about naturally if you work on the last ability – to be able to pick and play notes from a set you know will sound good over the chord being played. These "sets" are the tones of the chord itself and the scales that jibe with it. In this method, you learn three such scales: the major scale in the key you're playing, the blues scale in that key and the blues scale in a related key. Acquiring the ability to select and play notes from those scales involves developing knowledge in your head as well as the muscle memory needed to coax the notes from your instrument expeditiously. The Garage Band method is just a way to acquire that knowledge and muscle memory by playing music and having fun, rather than through grueling drills.

3

THE BLUES, HARD-WIRED INTO OUR SUBCONSCIOUS

We base this teaching method on the blues because the blues is America's national "folk" music. Forget the usual use of the term folk music – which has come to mean the kind of songs Peter, Paul and Mary sang at hootenannies back in the Sixties. Think instead of today's mass culture as purveyed in recordings, on radio, television and in the movies. That's where you find the real music of American folk. Our country buys millions of recordings a year. The vast majority of them are the blues or its offspring – rock, rap, heavy metal, country, reggae, movie themes, show tunes, jazz, etc.

The beat of the blues is the beat by which America lives. Even if you don't buy CDs or listen to the radio, you haven't escaped the blues. They ride the elevator with you, courtesy of Muzak. They stroll along behind you at Walmart, the grocery store and Bloomingdales, beamed at you through speakers hidden in the ceiling. They talk to you on the phone when you're put on hold. They smack you in the face at the movies. They tap their foot on your living room carpet every time you crank up the television. Some of us even hear blues at church.

Most Americans under the age of 50 have a blues groove drummed into the nether regions of their subconscious. You can tap that resource to become a player instead of a listener.

Dennis Cleary, the harmonica player in our band, had never played piano or keyboard. After two lessons with Ken Harris, the blues pianist who helped write the piano chapters in this book, Dennis started jamming on rhythm piano at band practice. Now, four months later (June 1995), he plays keyboards on half our tunes – at practice and in gigs. "It's pretty cool how simple the whole thing is if you look at it the right way," he says.

Dennis Cleary

How the Blues "Work"

As luck would have it, the quality that gives the blues universal appeal also makes blues a perfect teaching tool. That's how we use the blues in this book, as a tool, not an end. We're not here just to teach you to play blues. We use the blues to teach you how to play any music.

Music "works" by creating and resolving various kinds of tension, much the way conflict in a movie or novel creates tension. A good movie plot may be humorous, romantic or thrilling, but it always revolves around some kind of conflict that creates tension in the viewer. The writer, actors and director must resolve that tension somehow. The lost lovers have to find each other, or the detective must identify the murderess. Whatever the plot, when the viewer gets to the end, he or she wants to heave a sigh of satisfaction at a successful conclusion in which the elements of the story come together and make sense.

That's the way with most successful music, too. The sounds of a tune take us up or down, in and out, away and back again, then return us to ground zero with a tear, a laugh, a sigh, or a thumping heart. Most music – except that of the avant garde, cliff-hanger variety – also leaves us with a sense of completeness, a sense that all avenues have been explored. The reason the blues is one of the simplest and most popular forms of music to play or sing is that most of the people in our rock 'n' roll culture can intuitively resolve the musical issues created by combinations of "blue" notes.

In music, discord creates tension through the "clashing" of tones. We put quotes around clashing because there are various levels of discord. At one end of the spectrum are the tone combinations (chords) that sound terrible. They really clash. They make us wince. We want to get away from them. At the other end are tone combinations that sound "nice." We feel comfortable with them. In between are combinations that sound mysterious or provocative, bluesy or romantic, religious or militaristic. Some are simple, some are erudite, but all create a tension that wants relieving, a tension that creates a need for something more, a need for movement to **another** combination of tones, then another and another and, finally, to a combination of tones that creates a sense of finality and no longer suggests movement.

The job of musicians is to move from one combination of tones to another along an "appropriate" path to reach a satisfying conclusion – appropriate meaning that the movement sounds good and evokes the desired emotions from the listeners.

In the most complex music – classical compositions and bebop jazz – the possible routes from Point A to Point B to Point C in a tune are numerous because subtle chords create subtle tensions that can lead in numerous directions. At every juncture, the classical composer or improvising jazzist must make choices that affect the direction the music moves. Understanding those choices and playing them in an effective manner requires a lot of study and knowledge.

The beauty of blues as a vehicle for learning to improvise on a musical instrument is that the tensions created by playing any note of a blues scale at any point in a blues tune are not so subtle. They're blunt

Tom Moore plays lead guitar four or five nights a week in Boise's most popular blues band, Fat John and the Three Slims. He was the first music teacher not connected with this book to start using our method. He has used it successfully with guitar students in his community schools class and in private lessons at Old Boise Guitar Company. "I like it because it gets students playing and excited right away," he says.

Tom Moore

and to the point. Because of blues-based rock 'n' roll, blue notes are so much a part of our cultural heritage, our mass consciousness, that they go right to our gut or heart. We don't have to think about them. Something inside us knows intuitively where the music should go next – and next and next – to eventually resolve the tension. If we listen, we can hear the directions in our heads. Our conscious minds may not know the way, but our ears and instincts do. When we start playing notes from a blues scale over the chord changes of a blues tune, we intuitively start forming licks and riffs that sound cool to us.

Learning to play blues simply means teaching our fingers to make an instrument follow the subconscious lead of our ears and instincts, which, it turns out, is easier and a lot more fun for the beginner than teaching our fingers to follow more cerebral pathways.

4

GARAGE BAND BASICS
Part 1

The goal of the next several chapters is to tell you how you can acquire the knowledge and skills we've described in the previous chapters, enabling you to:

- Play the blues alone or with other musicians.
- Play other types of blues-based music, such as rock, country, reggae, etc.
- Use the blues as a tool to learn to play any kind of music.
- Know that with a reasonable amount of effort you can improve your playing to a shockingly high level.

How to Use this Material

The first step in this learning process is to read the following instructional chapters. The second step – if you believe what we say – is to find a teacher who meets the requirements described in the chapter on finding a teacher. We **strongly** recommend you study with a teacher. That's the fastest, easiest way to learn. If you can't afford a teacher, you will have to find substitutes. The best substitute is a musician friend who can show you the stuff we describe. If you can't find and cultivate a musician friend, the next best (a distant third) substitute is a combination of video tapes, audio tapes, CDs and books. There are lots of good materials. Later, we'll tell you how to find them.

The final step is to give this book to the teacher, telling him or her that you want to be taught by our method. The teacher may not have heard of us, but if he or she has the skills to teach this way, then he or she will understand the method and be able to use it. As we've said before, our method is simply the bare essentials of the way most accomplished rock, blues, country and jazz players learned to improvise at some point. The difference is that most of them scouted out the path themselves, exploring many side roads that used up a lot of time.

The Plan in a Nutshell

Here's the basic plan. The teacher will teach you how to play a six-note blues scale on your instrument. Once you can do that, he will give you a recording of a rhythm section (usually a piano or guitar, a bass and drums) playing a 12-bar blues. Then he will show you how to improvise (groove) along with the recording in a simple way, using a few notes from the blues scale. At that point, the teacher will send you home to play and have fun with that small bit of knowledge. You'll go home, experiment and discover that when you let go of your inhibitions you can suddenly make simple, but cool, music. You will come back the next week ready to learn more.

That's essentially what you'll be doing through the Garage Band basic plan. Within the framework described in this and the following chapters, the teacher will introduce easily digestible chunks of new knowledge as you need them. His or her role is to lead you through the routine described in this book, observe your playing and show you how to improve it a little each week. One week the teacher may help you with rhythm, another with technique, tone or musicality. That will depend on the teacher's judgment about you and your immediate needs. You will progress because you'll have fun.

After the second or third week, you will be able to play blues with recordings or other people – if you try. By the end of the basic plan, you will be able to play blues with anybody – in all 12 keys. You can complete the basic plan in from six months to a year and a half, depending on the instrument you play, your ability, your teacher's ability and how much you practice. At that point, you also will possess a foundation of musical knowledge, skills and confidence that will empower you to learn to play not just blues, but whatever kind of music you want with whatever kind of ensemble you want.

This Learning Method is Tried and True

As we said earlier, this learning method is the same as that used by little children to learn to speak their native languages. It is the same way tens of thousands of people have learned to play blues and rock guitar. It works.

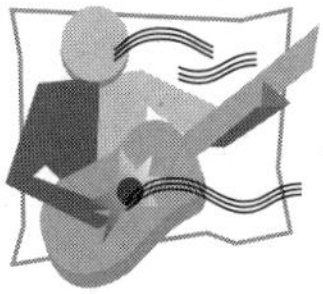

Why Use Our Method Instead of the Teacher's?

You may wonder why you should use our method if you're going to hire a teacher who probably has his or her own perfectly good way of teaching. That's a fair question. The answer has to do with the fact that music teachers don't go to school to learn how to give private lessons. They wing it. Most end up using a classical approach, which is how they learned themselves, starting out by reading notes on a page. They were able to learn that way because they are tougher, more disciplined or more talented than most people. It's a hard way to go. Stay away from people

A Note to Teachers about Our Rash Statements Concerning How Most Jazz, Blues and Rock Musicians Learned to Improvise

Some teachers and players are likely to quibble with our assertion that most improvisers learned their skills by the method we describe. Obviously, a lot of teachers — horn and piano players in particular — didn't start out their musical careers improvising, as we suggest doing. They may, for example, have started out reading music in school band or under a piano teacher. If so, they began improvising later. When they did, they had to do what we describe here — using simple riffs and patterns to create a groove.

Of course, they may have learned to groove alone instead of with a recorded rhythm section, as we suggest. But if they did that, we'll bet they were lucky enough to have play-along tapes going in their heads.

Of course, they may not have used the blues scale to improvise, as we suggest, either. We are well aware that many guitarists, for example, use the minor pentatonic scale. Other people use major scales or modal scales. But that's beside the point. They still employ a few notes from some scale to form riffs and patterns and work them into a groove. They have to — because that's the only way to do this stuff.

Of course, if you still want to argue, you may point out that not every improviser starts out using the 12-bar blues form, which we suggest, but that's also beside the point. Whether you start with a different blues or rock chord progression or leap past those simple forms into more complex jazz chord progressions, every improviser still has to work riffs and patterns into a groove.

All we're saying is that the essence of the process is the same in every case. You can substitute a pentatonic scale for the blues scale. You can use another progression instead of the 12-bar form. Or you can throw students into more complicated licks if they already possess some technical ability, but the basic task will always be the same.

who teach that way unless your primary goal is to read music. They will start you out reading music and playing simple tunes like *Twinkle Twinkle Little Star* that aren't much fun. Even if you stick out this process and get better, you'll still just be able to read music, which is a slow, clunky way to do things until you play extremely well. You won't be able to improvise at all. That's a drag because most of the music we all like and listen to on the radio and CDs – rock, country, blues, jazz, reggae, grunge, punk, rap, heavy metal, etc. – is improvised. You can't play rock or blues or country by reading music – not the way they're supposed to be played. So, why not learn to do what you like – improvisation – since it's easier, comes naturally and is more fun?

Why Should a Teacher Use Our Method?

The kind of teacher you want is a rock, blues, country or jazz musician who plays improvised music. Our chapter on how to find a teacher tells you how to locate and identify such people. The search process is part of a self-fulfilling prophecy. If you follow our instructions and track down a person capable of teaching you to improvise, we're pretty sure he or she will look at our method and say, "Sure, that's a good way to teach." The bet is rigged, because the ideal teacher we describe is an accomplished blues, rock, country or jazz player who at some point in his or her career learned to improvise in more or less the same manner described in this book. There isn't any other way to learn to improvise. All we've done is systematize and distill it to the essentials.

We're betting that teachers with the qualities we prescribe will appreciate what we've done here because, right now, most of them are making up their own methods as they go. They struggle on their own, trying to find the best way to teach students things that took them many years to learn. Our method can make that job easier, which we believe most of them will appreciate because teaching is not their first love. They're musicians. They teach because they need money.

The "Lessons"

We put quotation marks around the word lessons, because the written material we discuss isn't composed of lessons in the traditional sense. The real lessons are what the teacher tells you and demonstrates for you. The written materials described in this chapter are tool kits to help you remember and learn what the teacher explains and what you discover for yourself.

You will note that each of the tool kits includes written music. Please don't be alarmed. Although our method abandons the traditional approach of teaching you to play by reading music, we still think it is important to promote reading as a sideline, another tool in the kit. Specifically, we introduce written music:

- So we can illustrate our musical ideas, giving you something to show your teacher and say, "I want to be taught like this."
- Because when you learn some music by ear, you remember better if you can refer back to written notes.
- Because many of you already know how to read music.

Publishing the "Tool Kits"

We plan to write and publish lesson books for different instruments to provide the written materials described for each lesson. They will include our musical tool kits. However, you need not wait for those conveniences. Any teacher worth his or her salt can write out the materials we describe in a few minutes. This is not rocket science.

5

GARAGE BAND BASICS Part 2

If you are by nature an inflexible person, you may be disappointed to find that the following sections are not written out as cookbook instructions. They're not written that way because we don't want you to learn how to bake one kind of cake. We want you to learn how to cook anything you want to eat. Really learning to play a musical instrument is a personal experience involving you and other people. Your experience will be different than mine or Bob's or anybody else's, because you're different. There is no single recipe. Keeping that in mind, we start with a narrative of what probably would take place if you wanted to play the saxophone and could take lessons from Bob. We begin with the sax – even though we know more people want to learn to play piano or guitar – because the sax is simpler than piano or guitar, so it's easier to explain basic principles with the sax. Don't worry. In later chapters, we'll explain how you can translate the narrative on the sax to fit the guitar, piano and other instruments.

The Situation

So, for now, imagine you want to learn to play tenor sax and live with us in Boise, Idaho, a lovely city that sits at the foot of one mountain range and looks across a broad valley to another. Here's the scene: For years you've toyed with the idea of learning to play the saxophone.

Then, a couple of months back, your Uncle Ray died and left you the old King tenor he used to play in dance bands when he was younger. Overcome with fond memories of your sweet old uncle, you decided you'd give the horn a try in his honor. You began looking for a qualified teacher. After several weeks of scouting the city, you've finally identified a likely prospect. His name is Bob, and his trio plays jazz at a bar downtown. That's where you tracked him down, talked to him between sets and made an appointment for a lesson.

How to Use this Narrative

As you read the description of a student learning to play the sax,try to imagine yourself in the student's situation. If you want to play the piano instead of sax, think how the discussion might apply to the piano. If you know more about music than the novice we describe, think about how your knowledge might help you to move along more quickly.

Lesson 1

The first time you visit Bob's living room studio, you find two kitchen chairs set up in front of Bob's stereo. His old Selmer tenor sax sits in a stand beside one of the chairs. He can see you feel awkward, so he makes a joke to put you at ease while you open up your sax case and put together Uncle Ray's lovely old tenor. Putting you at ease is important. Good music teachers, like good doctors, must have an excellent bedside manner. Learning is like healing. You can't do it if you're uptight and doubtful.

Bob watches you put the instrument together, making sure you do it right. Then he goes over the horn with you, showing you how it works and how to hold it correctly. Putting his mouthpiece on your horn, Bob plays up and down the scale from the lowest to the highest notes to make sure everything is in good repair. Handing it back, he nods approval, impressed that you had the good sense to have a repairman go through it the week before. He confirms the repairman's observation that your horn would probably bring $2,000 in a big city. You're lucky, he says. It's easier to learn on a good instrument. He also shows you his horn, a vintage Mark VI Selmer that cost him $700 a few years back. The horn of choice for professionals, it now is worth about $3,000 to $4,000 since Japanese real estate developers started collecting them. As the two of you converse, he watches you and listens to your comments closely, getting a fix on what you know and don't know about music and the saxophone.

When you finally sit down, he asks you what you want to learn. Being a clever sort, you do not say, "To play the sax." Instead, you reach for your shirt pocket and pull out your favorite David Sanborn tape already cued up to your favorite cut. "To play like this," you say. Bob puts the tape in the deck. While he listens to it, he keeps asking you questions.

"Do you play any other instruments?"

"A little guitar," you say.

"Do you read music?"

"No."

"Do you sing?"

"Only in the shower."

"Can you blow your horn?"

You tell him you can pick out *Mary Had a Little Lamb* by ear.

"That's good," he says, sounding like he really means it. "What kind of music do you listen to for fun?"

By the time David finishes the tune, Bob is starting to get a picture of who you are and what you want. That's half of this lesson – having Bob draw a bead on what you know so he can provide you the service you're paying him for. Since you've already told him you can play *Mary Had a Little Lamb,* he asks you to give it a try, which you do. It sounds terrible, of course, and for some reason you feel embarrassed at not being able to do something that most other people can't do either. Bob, however, just nods and says it's pretty neat that you picked that little tune out by ear. You're not sure what, but something about his manner makes you feel good, like you shouldn't worry about whether you played well or badly.

Do you have a fingering chart? he asks. (A fingering chart is a diagram of a sax that shows you which keys to hold down to play each note on the horn.) If you don't, he gives you one. You won't understand everything on it, since you don't read music, but the chart contains lots of valuable information and is pretty much self-explanatory. Look it over at home, he says, and don't worry about what you don't understand. It's just a tool that will help you as you progress.

Now, he picks up his own horn and starts talking about how to hold the mouthpiece between your lips and teeth. Just to show you how it works, he plays several lines out of your David Sanborn song, does a quick change of rhythm, tosses off a bluesy version of *Mary Had a Little Lamb,* and finishes up with some bibbity bop stuff that you vaguely recognize as bebop jazz. You both get a little laugh out of that. You're impressed, thinking, "This guy can play. Maybe he really can teach."

Now he makes you play again, holding your mouth the way he showed you. He talks to you about breath support and how you maintain it by blowing warm air from deep in your lungs. He shows you how to lay your fingers down on the keys one by one to go down to the low notes, then lift them up to go high. He talks to you about tone and what goes into the kind of tone that David Sanborn plays. He tells you how to take care of your instrument and how you get better only if you practice regularly.

Finally, he sends you home with instructions to just fool around with your horn a little bit every day, getting better acquainted with it, playing whatever notes you want. You don't get anything in writing for this lesson.

Here's what happened during Lesson 1

1. Bob learned what you want.
2. Bob learned what you can do.
3. Bob made sure your instrument is in good repair.
4. Bob taught you the basic mechanics of your instrument.
5. Bob showed you a little about how to get a good tone.
6. Bob put you at ease so you can focus on learning, not worrying about whether you measure up.
7. Bob won your confidence by playing a little fun music for you.

Warning: If your teacher doesn't do all these things the first lesson, be suspicious.

Lesson 2

The second time you come to Bob's living room studio, you'll find the same setup, the two chairs in front of the stereo and the sax nearby. This time, however, you'll also find a music stand in front of the chairs. On it will be a sheet of music paper with notes written on it. Don't confuse this sheet of paper with your lesson. They are two different things. The lesson is something you participate in – playing, asking questions and paying attention while Bob talks, plays and shows you stuff. Music is not about you and a piece of paper. It's about humans – you and the people you learn from and play with. The piece of paper is a tool kit to help you get more out of the lessons. Later, we will examine each of the tools in the kit.

The first part of this lesson does not even involve the piece of paper. In fact, it is much like the last lesson. First, Bob listens to you play your awkward tones – whatever you can play – watching to see how you do it and correcting your form if necessary.

Next, he teaches you how to play a G major scale by ear. If necessary, of course, he tells you that a major scale is the scale with which we're all familiar:

Do re mi fa so la ti do.

The G major scale is simply the one that starts on G and just happens to be the easiest to play on a saxophone because it is in the horn's midrange. (On a piano, the easiest is the key of C; on guitar, the easiest is A.) He shows you how to finger the notes, and you do it, blowing out your own **do re mi fa so la ti do**.

The Blues Scale

With the major scale quickly under your belt, he then teaches you the G blues scale. This, of course, takes a little more explanation, because most of us don't go around singing blues scales. For instance, he may explain that a scale is just a series of notes that are prescribed musical distances apart. There are lots of different scales used for different kinds of music and in different cultures. Think of the times you've heard the rather strange sounds of Japanese music in a movie. That music sounds the way it does because it's based on a Japanese scale that is strange to us, but not to Japanese people. For now, suffice it to say that a blues scale is one that combines the sounds of English folk music with the sounds of African folk music and involves several of what we have come to know as blue notes. It happens to be important in our culture because much of our popular music is based on it.

Bob teaches you the six notes of the blues scale by playing them for you, then showing you how to finger the notes. He then listens to you play them one by one. When he's done that, he finally gives you your first written tool kit. It is a single page of music paper containing the information shown on the following page.

Tool Kit for the Key of G

The sheet, of course, is all Greek to you since you don't read music. Knowing that, Bob immediately gives you another sheet he reserves for his beginning students. On it is written the following information about musical notation.

Basic Music Notation

The staff: The above system of five lines and four spaces is called a staff. The , symbol at the left end of the staff is called a treble clef. When a staff begins with a treble clef, the notes on each line or space have the names of the letters as shown above. There is another clef sign called a bass clef, but you don't need to know about that right now.

Bar Lines: The vertical lines on the staff are called bar lines. They break the music into units called **measures.**

Time Signature: The above symbol that looks like a fraction is called a time signature. This one is for "four-four" time, used in most blues. The top number is the number of beats in a measure. The bottom number indicates the type of note that is held for one beat, in this case a quarter note.

Flats: When a flat sign appears on a line or space of the staff, it means the note for that line or space should be lowered a half step.

Sharps: When a sharp sign appears on a line or space, it means the notes on that line or space should be raised a half step.

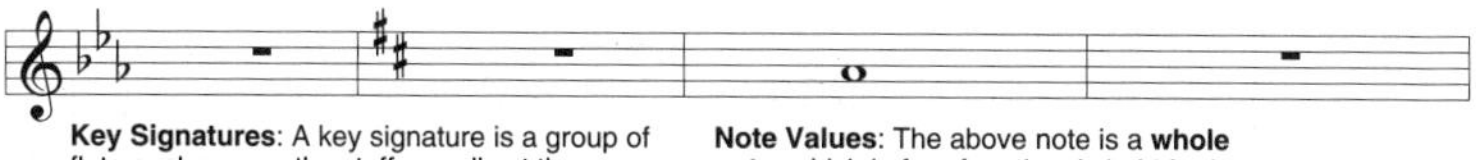

Key Signatures: A key signature is a group of flats or sharps on the staff, usually at the beginning of a tune. It not only tells you which notes are lowered or raised a half tone, it also tells you the key of the tune. (Right now you don't need to know how it does that.)

Note Values: The above note is a **whole note,** which in four-four time is held for four beats. The symbol in the next measure is a **whole rest,** which means you rest (don't play) for four beats.

Half Note: The note above is a half note held for two beats in four-four time. Beside it is a **half rest** , which means you rest for two beats.

Quarter Note: The quarter notes and **quarter note rests** shown above are held for one beat in four-four time.

Eighth notes: The eighth notes and **eighth note rests** shown above are held for half a beat in four-four time.

As he gives you this sheet of paper, Bob once again explains that he is not trying to teach you to read music right now. This is just another tool to help you understand and remember what you're learning by ear. With that in mind, he goes through the diagram of the treble staff with you, making sure you understand where the A is on the staff and that the names of the notes run from A through G sharp, then start over. That's all the musical notation you really need to know right now, just enough so you can sort of understand the written G major scale and the written blues scale.

Next, the two of you go through the first sheet of paper – the musical tool kit in the key of G, talking about each of the tools:

- **The G major scale:** This, of course, you know already. You learned it by ear 15 minutes ago. Now, Bob has you point to each of the notes and name them for him. If you have trouble, he has you write the letter of each note above it on the page. Finally, he has you look at the written notes as you and he play the scale together, starting to associate what you hear with what you see.
- **The G blues scale:** Again, Bob has you name each of the notes and, if necessary, write the letter of each note above it on the page. Again, you play the written notes, associating what you play and hear with what you see.
- **Two G scale patterns:** These are two little exercises made up of patterns of notes. If you call the notes of the scale 1, 2, 3, 4, 5 & 6, then a scale pattern might look like this 1 2 3 4, 2 3 4 5, 3 4 5 6, etc. Later, when the need arises, you'll want to use these exercises to help you get the scale under your fingers.

Not Freddie,
a small private joke

The title of our tool kit tune, *Not Freddie,* comes from the fact that the tune is not *Freddie Freeloader,* the Miles Davis blues standard that Bob and I would like to use in this book, but can't because the people who own the rights won't license it to us for some reason. Bob wrote *Not Freddie* so it harmonizes with *Freddie Freeloader*, which means you can have a lot of fun playing *Not Freddie* along with the original *Freddie* on Miles' *Kind of Blue* CD, the one jazz CD you should own if you don't own any others. (We recommend you buy it even though you'll be putting money in the pockets of the people who wouldn't license *Freddie Freeloader* to us in the first place. Just call us magnanimous.)

- **The 12-bar blues tune *Not Freddie* in G:** This is a melody, what most people call a tune and jazz or blues musicians call a "head." Jazz and blues musicians, he explains, play the head at the beginning of the performance, then improvise for a while, then finish the song by playing the head again. He'll teach you to play *Not Freddie* by ear on the third or fourth lesson. The written music is to help you learn and remember it.
- **The dorian and dominant scales:** You'll want to learn these two scales later to help you add some new sounds and variety to your improvising. Bob just puts them on the sheet now because they're part of the basic information about the key of G.
- **The G major seventh, G minor seventh and G dominant seventh chords:** These are the basic chords with the note G as a root. You'll need them later, too. Right now all you need to know is that a chord is two or more notes played together to create a particular kind of sound and feeling. (Music theorists will quibble with this definition, but it works for our purposes here.) Obviously, you can't play more than one note at a time on the sax, but eventually you'll play with other people. One of your goals then will be to ensure that the note you play makes the right chord with the notes your partners are playing. For now, however, don't worry about chords. They are on the sheet for later reference.

Once he explains all this, Bob goes through the G major and G blues scales with you again, playing them while you refer to the written notes. Then he makes **you** play the scales, following the written notes. He also reminds you that the fingering chart for your horn displays this information and more about musical notation. You may want to refer to it at home. (By now, of course, a lot of students will have studied the fingering chart at home anyway.)

A Note on Using Recorded Rhythm Sections

We obviously think you should buy and use our Garage Band CD because it is the best play-along option for beginners on the market. Just in case you're skeptical, here's the lowdown on all your options.

CDs: Compact Discs are the best choice for most people for several reasons. First of all, they're always in tune because their tones don't depend on the speed of the player. If you use a play-along tape and your tape player runs at a different speed than the one on which the tape was made, then the pitch you hear on your machine will not be accurate and you may not be able to match it with your instrument. That won't happen with a CD. The other nice feature of a CD is that you can cue it quickly to play the cut you want. Rewinding tapes is a pain when you're playing one cut over and over again. There are a several blues play-along CDs on the market. We think ours is best because it is all 12-bar blues, has the simplest blues chord changes and is recorded so the chord changes are easy to hear.

Records and Tape Cassettes: You can save a few bucks by purchasing a play-along tape instead of a CD, but we don't recommend it. If you want to break the law, heaven forbid, you can save even more by copying a friend's CD, but we don't recommend that either. If your machine runs faster than the one on which the copy was made, it will make the tones sharp; running slower will make them flat. Even if you can match the tone, you'll be training your ear to play out of tune. You may be lucky and have a turntable or tape player that runs at the right speed, but you'll need a variable-speed machine to make certain the playback will be in tune with your instrument. Such players are expensive and hard to find used. Take our advice: if you own a CD player, buy a CD.

Band in a Box: The most versatile play-along option is a computer program called Band in a Box, which is produced by PG Music and is available in hip music stores as well as from mail order houses. If you have a computer with a sound card and a stereo system to play it through, then Band in a Box will play 12-bar blues (or other tune forms) in any key and a host of rhythmic styles. It's great and is always in tune because it's digital.

The CD and Rhythm Section

That said, Bob drops a CD into the player. This, he tells you, is the basic Garage Band CD, which you can buy from him, by mail or at your favorite music store. It contains:

- Some tuning notes so you can tune your horn to the CD.
- Play-along versions of a rhythm section playing 12-bar blues in all 12 keys.

Bob runs the CD through the tuning notes and shows you how to tune your horn to them, so that when you play along you'll be able to play at the same pitch as the stereo. Then he plays the first cut, which is a rhythm section – guitar, bass and drums – playing the bass line and chords of a 12-bar blues in G, but no melody.

As a rhythm section, the guitar, bass and drums do a couple of things. Obviously, they set up a rhythm and maintain the tempo (or speed) of the tune for the rest of the band (you, in this case). The other job of the rhythm section is to maintain the skeleton of the tune, the chord progression we discussed in Chapter 2. Usually, the rhythm guitar (or piano) creates this skeleton by playing the full chord in rhythm, moving from chord to chord as the band moves through the tune. The bass moves from chord tone to chord tone within each chord.

After providing you this long-winded explanation, Bob hits the CD player and starts the G blues again. This time he plays along with the rhythm section, playing the head to *Not Freddie*, then improvising some simple, but pretty, blues licks. (A lick or riff is a short musical statement.) This, he explains, is what you soon will be doing. Then he sells you the Garage Band CD at a very reasonable price. He doesn't really say much more about it at this point. He just wants you to have it, know what's on it and to listen to it during the week. Finally, he sends you home with instructions to practice both your scales each day. He promises that next week you will begin playing music.

Here's what happened during Lesson 2

1. Bob listened to you play any tones you could. If necessary, he corrected your form.
2. He taught you the G major and G blues scales by ear.
3. He explained the first musical tool kit, the one for the key of G.
4. He checked your knowledge of written music and, since you don't read, provided you a brief fact sheet on musical notation.
5. He explained that a chord is two or more notes played together to create a particular musical feeling or tension.
6. He taught you how to tune your horn to the play-along CD .
7. He played the recorded G blues rhythm section on the play-along CD , talked to you about the function of a rhythm section and sold you a Garage Band CD to take home for your very own.

Lesson 3

This is a good week for you, musically speaking. You're a little lonesome because your live-in lover is out of town, but that leaves you lots of time to practice your sax. You put in at least 30 minutes every night. So, when you arrive at Bob's, you're ready. You know your G major scale, the G blues scale and even a few more notes, which you learned off your fingering chart. They're even getting a bit easier to blow.

When Bob asks you to play, you knock the two scales off boom boom boom and sit back waiting for the applause. Bob nods, smiles and gives you a hearty, "All right." Bob isn't a real demonstrative guy, but, like any good teacher, he's proud when a student practices and makes use of a lesson. (Conversely, he's disappointed when a student shows up and has not practiced, which happens with everybody once in a while.)

You're the kind of student he likes. You're making good progress. You know the G blues scale and you seem to be relaxed, enjoying the process. That's the important part for Bob, having fun. Your embouchure – the way you hold the mouthpiece in your mouth – is shaping up, and your tone sounds pretty good. There are things Bob could criticize, but what's the point? You're here to have fun. More criticism at this point is more likely to hurt than to help. Besides, you're ready for the big leap – into the blues.

Your Introduction to Grooving

Before you arrived, Bob had put his Garage Band CD into the player. Now he turns it on and the two of you tune your horns to the tuning notes at the beginning. Then he stops the CD. What you're going to do right now is learn to groove, he says. First without the CD, then with it. At your level, he explains, grooving is the most important part of music, simply because it's fun and you can do it without knowing much. What you're going to do first, he says, is play a game of call and response. He'll call – play a note or two on his horn – and you'll respond in rhythm by repeating whatever he did.

How can you do that? you ask. Your ear's not that good. Sure it is, he says. Besides, you can watch his fingers on the keys, too. It's only two notes. If he's feeling particularly garrulous, Bob may even explain that the blues version of this game came over on slave ships from Africa. You may remember it from one of those old chain-gang movies where the leader of a railroad work gang leads a song and the gang driving spikes responds:

Leader:	Swing on down boys.
Gang:	Swing on down boys.
Leader:	WHACK it mighty hard now.
Gang:	WHACK it mighty hard now.
Leaders:	Swing on down boys.
Gang:	Swing on down boys ... etc.

If you don't recall that, surely you remember the cheerleader at your alma mater, Bad News High School, leading cheers at football games:

Cheerleader:	We're from Bad News.
Crowd:	We're from Bad News.
Cheerleader:	Mighty mighty Bad News.
Crowd:	Mighty mighty Bad News ... etc.

Bob will do exactly the same thing as the chain gang and cheerleaders, except he will blow his horn instead of shouting or chanting. Also, the call will be simpler. He'll limit himself to the first two notes of the blues scale. (For our little description here, we're going to call the first note Tah and the second one Pah.)

Bob gets ready for the game by counting to establish a rhythm, ONE two three four, ONE two three four... , making you count along and tap your foot to get the feel for the beat.

Then he plays and counts. You respond and count.

Him:	TAH two three four.
You:	TAH two three four.
Him:	TAH two three four.
You:	TAH two three four.
Him:	Tah Pah Three four
You:	Tah Pah Three Four
Him:	Tapa two three four.
You:	Tapa two three four.
Him:	TAH papa three four.
You:	TAH papa three four.
Him:	Tapa papa three four.
You:	Tapa papa three four ... etc.

How to Read This Exercise

The adjacent exercise will make more sense if you will read the call and response aloud and in rhythm.

You're scared at first, afraid you won't be able to follow and pass this first test of your musical worthiness. (You're a fairly quick person, but still are hindered by the screwed-up middle class American idea that everything you do is competition and has to be measured against what others can do.) After a couple of tries, however, you realize you can do it. You get into it: Tah papa three four, Tah papa three four, Tapa tapa three four, Tapa tapa three four.

You like it. You're grooving. You and Bob, just two saxophones playing two notes and, gosh, it sounds neat. Your tone even sounds better, no longer awkward, somehow musical just because you're playing in rhythm.

Trading Twos

In fact, you have so much fun that you're disappointed when Bob stops. You perk up again when he says, "Yeah. You've got it. That's the way to do it." You're ready to improvise along with the CD. What you're going to do, he explains, is "trade twos," which means he's going to play two bars, then you'll play two bars. Then he'll play two more, et cetera and so forth. A bar, he explains is four beats, the basic unit of rhythm in the blues. But don't worry about that right now. If you're not sure when to come in, Bob will tell you. Also, it's not going to be call and response this time. You don't have to do what Bob does. Just do whatever you want, playing one, two or three notes of the blues scale any way you want. The important thing is to get the feel of the music and play in rhythm.

He starts the CD and the band leader counts out the tempo: One and Two and One Two Three Four. The piano, bass and drums start, doo-bie, doo-bie, doo-bie ... and Bob chimes in with his sax, Tah pah pah pah, tah pah pah pah.

As he finishes, he gives you the nod. You're on. You're nervous, too, feeling as though you're on the stage at Carnegie Hall, frozen stiff before 2,000 people, listening to the rhythm section come into your part, doobie, doobie, doobie, doob ... Amazingly – you do it: Tah two three four, Pah two three four. Bob chimes in again: Tah papa tah pah, Tah papa tah pah ... This time you're ready for the nod and play: TAH pah TAH pah, TAH pah TAH pah right along with the band.

As Bob plays again, you're getting the feel. This time you know when to come in: Tah pah Tah pah, Tah pah Tah pah.

You've forgotten your white middle class roots. You're playing music now. Bob, seeing you relax, loosens up and adds another note and rhythm to his lick: Tapa Deeeeeeee Pah, Tapa Deeeeeeee Pah. You take the challenge and throw in another note, too: Tapa Doooooooo Pah, Tapa Doooooooo Pah. It's not the same note as Bob, but who cares? It sounds cool. (You know it does, because Bob laughs when he hears it.) He comes back with his same lick: Tapa Deeeeeeee Pah, Tapa Deeeeeeee Pah. This time you get it, too: Tapa Deeeeeeee Pah, Tapa Deeeeeeee Pah. Bob laughs again. He's having as much fun as you are. This time he plays: Tapa Deeeee Pah Dee, Tapa Deeeee PahDee. And you do it, too: Tapa Deeeee Pah Dee, Tapa Deeeee Pah Dee, thinking, this isn't so hard.

How to Tell What Key a Song is In

With most popular kinds of recorded tunes, it is easy to figure out what key the players are playing. All you do is listen to the last note of the song and try different notes on your instrument until you match that final note. If a C matches it, then the tune is being played in C. If a D matches it, then it's in D, etc., etc. This methods works nine times out of 10 with rock, blues, country, folk, etc. kinds of songs.

Feeling the Beat

By the time the rhythm section runs seven times through the blues progression and quits, you've got the concept down. You're playing two- and three-note licks like nobody's business. You're doing it in time. You're feeling the beat. And you're listening to how it sounds. Most of the time, it sounds neat. You're playing music – not from notes written on paper, not memorized from something Bob told you, but out of your own head and body.

Bob starts the CD over, and you do it again, getting more confident as you go. Then he runs it back again and says you're ready for the next step, trading "fours," i.e. four bars instead of two. The task is the same. You just get to make a longer musical statement when you play. (You're thinking: Did I make some musical statements? Wow. I guess I did, if Bob says so.)

During a pause, Bob gives you some other exciting news. You can, he says, play the way you've just been playing along with **any** 12-bar blues in the key of G. That means, you can play along with **any** 12-bar blues because any 12-bar blues can be played in G or any other key if you can get somebody to do it with you.

By the time you run through the CD twice more, trading fours, you're starting to get a feel for the longer phrases and are thinking: Just let me get home with my own CD in the privacy of my own living room and I'll figure out how to do this right. I can do this. I can play every 12-bar blues tune in the world. As you think these thoughts, you have just been sucked into the current of the Garage Band river. You're caught. We've got you. Unlike most music students, you are fantasizing about doing the one thing that will surely make you a better musician – practice.

1. Bob listened to you play what you learned last week (your G scales) and corrected your form if necessary.
2. You learned to groove with your horn by playing call and response with Bob.
3. By grooving, you learned you can make surprisingly musical music using two or three notes and playing in rhythm (with emphasis on playing in rhythm).
4. You learned to groove along with the CD by trading twos and fours with Bob.
5. You learned that you can play along with any 12-bar blues by doing what Bob has shown you.

Here's what happened during Lesson 3

Lesson 4

This turns out to be not such a good week for you musically. Your live-in, Jane (Jack), comes home from her (his) vacation, is understandably grumpy at the prospect of returning to work and, all in all, doesn't feel inclined to nurture your musical growth if it means listening to you practice more than once every five or six weeks. She (he) banishes you, your horn and your CD to the garage. (Fortunately, it's summer and you have a ghetto blaster on which to play the CD.)

As this point in your new musical career, you begin to realize that adding music to your life is like adding anything else of substance. Before music, you had reached an equilibrium of some sort. You filled each day with various combinations of work, play, relationships and rest. Now you're trying to fit music into that same 24 hours. Not surprisingly, you have to make trade-offs. Jane (Jack), of course, likes the idea of you playing the sax. She's (he's) an enlightened and supportive babe (dude). But the reality of sax practice in the next room would try anyone's nerves.

You have solved the current domestic problem by retreating to the garage, but after a while it will dawn on Jane (Jack) that for a part of every evening you're out there with your sax and ghetto blaster instead of snuggling up with her (him) on the couch watching the nightly news like you used to do. Pretty soon you'll also meet up with some guitar players and start holding band practice every Sunday afternoon instead of mountain biking with Jane (Jack) – like you used to do. Of course, Jane (Jack) won't think of it as band practice. She'll (he'll) think of it as you and your buddies getting together to drink beer and have fun while she (he) sits home alone. (If you're a woman, Jack will fear you're having an affair with one of the guitar players. Men are incredibly paranoid about things like that.)

You need to be aware of these potential problems, but please don't panic. There are alternatives to telling Jane (Jack) to pack up and get out. As we said, you short-circuit the domestic problems this week by retreating to the garage, where you put in a good half hour each night, improvising along with the CD. One night you spend a whole hour there, blowing your brains out for the lawn mower, the work bench and mountain bikes. By the end of the week, you're starting to develop some licks of your own. You're grooving. You've even read the fingering chart and are starting to extend your playing range above and below the one octave of the G blues scale that Bob taught you. (An octave is the part of a scale between two G's, two A's, B's, etc.)

When you stroll into Bob's living room this week, you're feeling cool. He asks you to play your scales, and you knock them cold. He puts on the CD to trade fours, and you wail. When the CD finishes, you're hoping he'll run it back so you can play some more. You understand that what you're doing is crude, but it's fun, particularly when you're playing with someone as good as Bob. Moreover, Bob's body language tells you he once again is pleased with your progress. He's good at giving attaboys (girls) without actually saying anything.

Unfortunately, what he says in the English language is that it's time to learn something new. That's another part of this philosophy: Always have the student working on two things, something familiar and something that pushes him (her). Today, Bob's going to push you with your first tune, *Not Freddie,* a blues tune he wrote to harmonize with Mile Davis' *Freddie Freeloader.*

You spend most of the rest of the lesson on the tune. First Bob plays it for you while you try to follow the notes on the written page he gave you last week. The tune is not really your style, but you like it. It's simple and cool. Once you've heard it, Bob makes you try to play along with him.

He teaches you the tune a phrase at a time, so you can do it by ear. He plays a phrase while you watch his fingers. Then you play it. If you make a mistake, he tells you what you did wrong. Then he plays it again and you do, too – right this time. Then he plays the next phrase, and you repeat the process. Pretty soon, you begin to realize that the phrases repeat themselves. You mention that to Bob, and he gives you a gold star, explaining that that's the way of most blues tunes. In *Not Freddie,* for example, there's one phrase that's played exactly the same three times. Two other phrases are similar to the repeated phrase. Then there are two phrases played just once. The whole tune is just five phrases. That's the beauty of the blues, he explains. They're simple.

By the end of the lesson, you're playing *Not Freddie* all the way through, albeit roughly, thinking this beats the heck out of *Mary Had a Little Lamb*. You're not really reading the tune from the page, but do find yourself referring to the page when you can't remember the next note you're supposed to play.

To finish up, Bob puts the CD on, so the two of you can play *Not Freddie* along with it. By the second time through, you're thinking: I can do this. If I go home and practice in the privacy of my own garage, I'll be able to do this by next week. (As we said earlier, you're falling into a practice routine. If you're not careful, you'll soon be playing 15 hours a day, as Charlie Parker did during parts of his brief but white-hot career.)

Bob interrupts your thoughts as you're packing to leave, "Oh, yeah," he says. "It's time."

"Time for what, you say?" you ask.

"Time to find somebody to play with."

"I've only had four lessons," you say.

"I know," he says, "but you can play with me and the CD, so you can play with somebody else. Find a guitar player. That's the best."

Since he doesn't have another student scheduled, the two of you talk for a few minutes about how to find a novice guitar player who's at or near your level of playing.

"I don't know if I'm ready," you say.

"Just do it," he says. "If you do find somebody now, you'll get better fast, and you'll play music all your life."

1. Bob listened to you play what you learned last week (improvising on the G blues scale along with the CD) and corrected your form if necessary.
2. You learned to play your first blues tune, *Not Freddie*, by ear.
3. You learned a little more about reading music by referring to the written page to keep from getting lost while you played *Not Freddie.*
4. Bob told you it's time to find someone to make music with.

Here's what happened during Lesson 4

Lesson 5

This week's not such a good one for practice. Your pal Charlie flies up from L.A. for the weekend, which blows your two big practice days. To make matters worse, Tuesday night is Jane's (Jack's) birthday, so you have to take her (him) out to dinner. By the time your lesson rolls around on Wednesday, you've hardly played *Not Freddie*. Naturally, the first thing you do when you walk into Bob's is apologize for this, which is kind of funny since you're the one paying for the lessons.

Despite your apology, Bob remains fairly unsympathetic **and** unconcerned, which surprises you because you remember the guilt trip your teachers laid on you back in school when you didn't do your homework. What you may not realize is that Bob really believes what's in this book. He has taught long enough to know that you either will practice or you won't. He knows he couldn't make you practice even if he tried. No outside force can. You're a free, self-supporting adult. You do what you like. Bob understands that all he can do is show you how practice will help you have more fun playing music. The only thing that can **make** you practice is an internal force – your own desire to create whoopee with a saxophone.

To hear for himself how much or little you've done, he asks you to play *Not Freddie.* You get through it okay, though you know you could do it more smoothly if you'd only had time to practice over the weekend when you were out playing golf with Charlie. Bob's only comment is to correct you once when you screw up the rhythm. He makes you play that part over until you do it right. Then he puts on the CD. You play *Not Freddie* together, then you trade fours, improvising until the end of the recording. You redeem yourself here, playing confidently, never straying from the blues scale. Stopping the CD, Bob nods his approving nod. You sound fine, he says.

Something Special Just for You

Bob is a little concerned about your tone, however, especially on your midrange D, so he is going to do what our method expects every teacher to do on occasion. He is going to provide you some custom instruction based on his personal observation of what you need right now to improve your playing of *Not Freddie.* At this point, another student might need help with rhythm or breath support, but what you need is a way to improve your tone by firming up your embouchure.

The difference between good tone and bad tone, Bob explains, is something that's easy to hear, but hard to express in words. Your tone, like that of most novices, is what Bob calls thin. It doesn't have enough meat or body. You want what saxophonists call a big, fat, round tone. To illustrate what he means, Bob asks you to play your G major scale. Then he plays the same notes, making them just as warm and fat and rich as he can. The difference is clear. Bob explains that he will show you how to work on that difference at home.

Before he does, however, he talks a little about your your midrange D being sharp (higher in pitch than it's supposed to be). He asks you to play up and down the G major scale again. You're not sure, but as you play this time, you think maybe you can hear the sharpness of the D yourself. It just doesn't quite fit it with the other notes in the scale.

That sharpness, Bob explains, is not all your fault. It's physically impossible to build a saxophone that's perfectly in tune with itself. The better the sax, the more in tune it will be, but even the best aren't perfect. Compromises have to be made by the designers. The midrange D is where the compromises often have their worst effect.

Part of learning to play a sax is learning to compensate for the horn's deficiencies by slightly adjusting your embouchure when you play a midrange D or other note that's out of tune. An accomplished player becomes married to her instrument, adjusting as she plays up or down the horn. (Put her on another, unfamiliar, horn, and she will play out of tune at first – until her ear prompts her body to adjust.)

Bob **could** tell you how to consciously adjust your pitch, by loosening or firming up your embouchure. (In case you've forgotten, embouchure is the way you hold your lips on a horn's mouthpiece.) That's not how it's done, however. You can't think fast enough to adjust your embouchure consciously when you're playing. What you need as a novice is an embouchure that on the conscious level is always the same, unwavering, solid. So he is going to give you a little exercise that will let you consciously pursue a solid embouchure while your subconscious helps you work on playing in tune.

It turns out your ear is the only teacher that can really tell your lips and body how to play in tune. And your ear will – in time. Your ear just doesn't like things to be out of tune. It likes harmony. It's similar to the poor dog in Professor Pavlov's famous experiment. Every time the dog ate from the wrong dish, he got an electric shock. Pretty soon he quit eating from that dish. Well, every time you hit that out-of-tune D, your ear gets a little jolt. So, it telegraphs a message to your lips, saying: You're sharp. You're sharp. Loosen up. Bring that pitch down.

To which your lips telegraph back: Bugger off. We're doing the best we can. Your ear, however, keeps calling back. And, over the months, as your lips get in better shape, they will grow more cooperative. Eventually they will follow your ear's orders – with little conscious help.

You can, however, speed up the process, Bob says. The way to do it is by playing long tones. He demonstrates, starting out on the G and playing each note of the major scale, holding each one for eight long beats, starting the note out soft, growing louder, then softer again. He repeats the routine on each note of the scale. Then he has you try it.

As you go up the scale, you discover the exercise quickly tires your lips. By the end, you're quavering like a 97-pound weakling on his twenty-fifth push-up. Good, Bob says. That's the idea. This exercise serves two purposes. One of them is exactly like doing push-ups. It's physical exercise. Long tones require your lips to strain. As they struggle, they grow stronger. As they grow stronger, they relax and let the reed vibrate more freely, generating the big, rich tone you seek.

In the meantime, your ear can hear problems with pitch more easily when you play those long, slow tones. As a result, your ear will become more insistent that your lips fix the sharpness of that recalcitrant D – which your new, stronger lips will do.

We Don't Believe in Preventive Maintenance

As we close out this section, it's worth noting that if you had been learning to play the sax under any of the traditional methods, you would have started your very first lesson playing the long-tone exercise Bob has just suggested. Under a traditionalist, you would have played long tones whether you needed them or not, even if you were one of the fortunate people who immediately fall into playing a fairly good tone. Instead of learning to groove first, as you have done, you would have spent your first practice sessions struggling with musical push ups. We don't believe in that.

In fact, we don't believe in preventive maintenance at all. Wait until a problem comes up, then fix it. That's our policy. If you started out playing long tones, you might ask yourself why you were doing it. They're a little bit hard to play and not pretty, nowhere near as much fun as grooving along with a CD. You might have said, "To heck with this," and quit. Now you're in a different place. You've played enough to see how long tones can help. Chances are you'll go home and play them quite a bit. One, because you've learned to have confidence in Bob's instruc-

Learning by Listening to Music

If you're going to play music, you need to spend a lot of time listening to the kind of music you want to play. While you're working through this method, you'll want to listen to blues in particular. Find tunes you like that feature great musicians playing simple lines on the instrument you're learning. Listen to those songs again and again, learning to sing and play the riffs you like, while building the "feel" of the tune into your subconscious and improving your ear.

tions. Two, because you're a musician now and want to do whatever you can to make your playing better and more fun.

Nagging Reminder

"Oh, yeah," Bob says as you're packing up. "Did you find yourself a guitar player?

You had been hoping he wouldn't ask. "Uh, no," you say, remembering the squeamish, little, cowardly feeling you've had all week at the thought of not only asking someone to play music with you, but of actually having to bare your musical soul to them if and when they accept your invitation.

"Just do it," he says, handing you a slip of paper. On it are written the name and phone number of a guitar teacher, a friend of his. "Call Ben and tell him to hook you up with one of his students."

All you can think is how difficult he's making it for you to **not** go looking for a partner.

1. Bob listened to you play and observed that it was time for you to start improving your tone.
2. You started learning about the difference between a thin, lifeless tone and a rich, fat tone.
3. You learned that some of the notes on a saxophone are never quite in tune with the others unless the player adjusts to make them so.
4. You learned how your ear can train your lips and body to adjust for the fact that the notes of a sax are never quite in tune with each other.
5. You learned a long-tone exercise that will help you consciously improve the quality of your tone at the same time your ear works on obtaining an accurate pitch.
6. Once again, Bob nagged you to find somebody to play with.

Here's what happened during Lesson 5

6

GARAGE BAND BASICS Part 3

We've now reached the point where the Garage Band process starts repeating itself. You've gone through one cycle, the one for the key of G. There are 12 cycles in all – one for each of the 12 keys. By now you've worked on the G blues for a month. You have this key pretty much under your fingers. What's important is not the number of weeks you spend on the key, but that Bob can see you've got a fairly good grasp of G blues. (We don't mean you have it perfected. We mean you have the key under control. It's a steer you've herded into the corral. You could try butchering and barbecuing the steer right now, but you really don't know enough about butchering and barbecuing steers to get the job done. What you want right now is to get some more steers in the corral. Then you can butcher and barbecue them all, once you know more about the nature of steers.)

Lessons 6 and 7

When you show up at Bob's for Lesson 6, he listens to the things you practiced the last week, makes observations as necessary, then introduces you to your next steer – the key of C. He teaches you the C major and C blues scales by ear and gives you your musical tool kit in C. That is to say, he repeats the process you went through in the beginning with the key of G. That process goes faster now because you've done it once and are getting better all the time. He also asks if you've called his guitar teacher friend, which you haven't.

When you show up for Lesson 7 a week later, he teaches you Thelonious Monk's *Blue Monk*, your blues tune in the key of C. You and he go through the same steps you went through with *Not Freddie*. Bob watches and corrects as necessary. Once again, relentless, he asks if you've called his guitar teacher friend, which you *still* haven't done because you've been *really* busy. (Yeah, right.)

Lesson 8

Your next big milestone comes at Lesson 8 after you've worked the C blues for two weeks. When you show up for this lesson, Bob has you play *Blue Monk* along with the CD, then improvise on C blues. You sound pretty good. You don't yet play *Blue Monk* the way Monk did, but, then, he wrote it. You do, however, practice a minimum of 20 minutes every day, and it shows. You have no trouble staying within the C blues scale as you play along with the CD.

Since you're doing so well, Bob says it's time to add more structure to your playing. As you may recall, you started with no structure. Your first lesson, you played whatever random notes you could blow. The next week, you added some structure by learning the G major scale. That same day, you learned the G blues scale.

The next week, you made a leap when you played "call and response" with Bob. In that one game, you learned to groove. You added the structure of rhythm to your playing. Things started cooking. At that same lesson, you began playing notes of the blues scale along with the rhythmic and harmonic structure of a recorded rhythm section – still more fun.

Today, Bob says, it's time to add the next level of structure to your music by learning how the blues form itself fits together.

The Mechanics of a Blues Tune

As Bob has said before, a tune hangs on a skeleton of chords. Complex tunes have lots of chords. Simple tunes have only a few. In either case, the principle is the same. The rhythm section plays chords in the background, while the soloist plays single notes that fit in with the chords as they flow by. Some of the soloist's notes will be actual chord tones. Others will be *passing* tones that aren't part of the chord, but sound good with the chord because they come from a scale in the key being played.

A basic 12-bar blues hangs on a skeleton of three chords. Your task in Lesson 8 is to understand each one of those chords and know when it's being played in the form. Once you do, you can start selecting and playing notes that go along with the chords.

What is most exciting about these three chords is that understanding how they work will allow you to play hundreds of rock, blues, pop, folk and country songs. They're called the I (One) Chord, the IV (Four) Chord and the V (Five) Chord because they're based on the first, fourth and fifth notes of the major scale in whatever key you're playing. Here's how they work – for hundreds of songs.

Look at the first verse of a song we hope you and most of our readers know, *See, See, Rider,* a traditional blues with many versions by many people over the last hundred or so years. It has three lines.

See, see, Rider. See what you done done ______________________.
See, see, Rider. See what you done done ______________________.
Made me love you. Now your man's done come ___________________.

Musically, this tune is exactly like hundreds of other 12-bar blues songs. Just to impress that fact upon you, Bob pulls out the following list, which shows a few of the many songs that are 12-bar blues.

A Few 12-Bar Blues Songs

Steam Roller	James Taylor
In the Mood	Glenn Miller
Before You Accuse Me	Eric Clapton;
	Credence Clearwater Revival
Black or White	Michael Jackson
St. Louis Blues	W.C Handy
Rock Around the Clock	Bill Haley and His Comets
I Feel Good	James Brown
Johnny B. Goode	Chuck Berry
Roll Over Beethoven	Chuck Berry; The Beatles
No Particular Place to Go	Chuck Berry
Good Golly Miss Molly	Little Richard
Pride and Joy	Stevie Ray Vaughn
Texas Flood	Stevie Ray Vaughn
Why Don't We Do It in the Road?	The Beatles
Got My Mojo Working	Muddy Waters; Elvis Presley
Your Mama Don't Dance And Your Daddy Don't Rock and Roll (Chorus Only)	Kenny Loggins and Jim Messina
Crossroads	Robert Johnson; Eric Clapton
Mustang Sally	Wilson Pickett; The Commitments
Money Blues	Bob Dylan
Move It on Over	Hank Williams Sr.; George
	Thorogood
Hound Dog	Elvis Presley; Big Mama Thornton
The Spider and the Fly	The Rolling Stones
Wipeout	The Surfaris
Stormy Monday	Allman Brothers; Bobby "Blue"
	Bland
Mr. PC	John Coltrane
Surf City	Jan and Dean
Born Under a Bad Sign	Homer Simpson; Albert King
Walking After Midnight	Cowboy Junkies
Honkey Tonk Blues	Hank Williams Sr.
Folsom Prison Blues	Johnny Cash
Sweet Home Chicago	Taj Majal; Robert Johnson
The Thrill is Gone	B.B. King
Red House	Jimi Hendrix
I Just Want to Make Love to You	The Rolling Stones; Muddy
	Waters; Foghat
Should I Stay or Should I Go?	The Clash

All these songs, he repeats, are musically just like *See, See, Rider*. In all of them, the band plays the I Chord all the way through the first line, as is shown below for the lyrics of *See, See, Rider*.

I Chord
See, see, Rider. See what you done done ________________________.

The band plays the IV Chord through the first half of the second line, then goes back to the I Chord for the second half of the line:

IV Chord **I Chord**
See, see, Rider. See what you done done ________________________.

On the third line, the band plays the V Chord through the first four beats, then the IV Chord for four beats, then goes back to the I Chord. If the song is ending, the I Chord continues through the end of the line. If the band is going to play another verse, it goes back to the V Chord at the end of the line as a "turn-around" to create the expectation of something more. It looks like this:

V Chord **IV Chord** **I Chord**
Made me love you. Now your man's done come ________________________.

Put it all together and it looks like the following:

I Chord
See, see, Rider. See what you done done ________________________.

IV Chord **I Chord**
See, see, Rider. See what you done done ________________________.

V Chord **IV Chord** **I Chord**
Made me love you. Now your man's done come ________________________.

Of course, to actually play a song, you have to pick out a particular key and learn the I, IV and V chords in that key. As we said, they are based on the first, fourth and fifth tones of the major scale in that key. To help you visualize this set-up, Bob writes out the C major scale with Roman numerals written below the notes like this:

C Major Scale

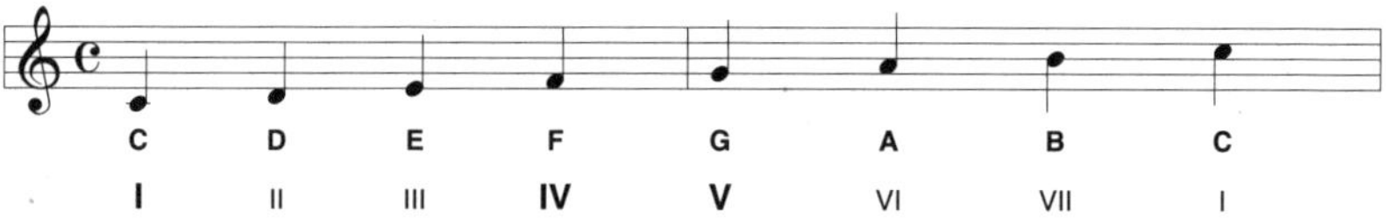

Seeing the scale, you quickly realize that in the key of C the I chord is the C chord, the IV chord is the F chord and the V chord is the G chord. So you can hear what the C chord sounds like, Bob sidles over to the piano and plays it, then the F and G chords.

Now he takes you back to *See, See, Rider,* which you now know looks as follows in the key of C.

I Chord (C Chord)
See, see, Rider. See what you done done ____________________.

IV Chord (F Chord) **I Chord (C Chord)**
See, see, Rider. See what you done done ____________________.

V Chord (G Chord) **IV Chord (F Chord)** **I Chord (C Chord)**
Made me love you. Now your man's done come __________________.

Each line of lyrics in a 12-bar blues corresponds to four bars of the music. So, if you look at the music for *See, See, Rider,* it looks like this:

See, See, Rider

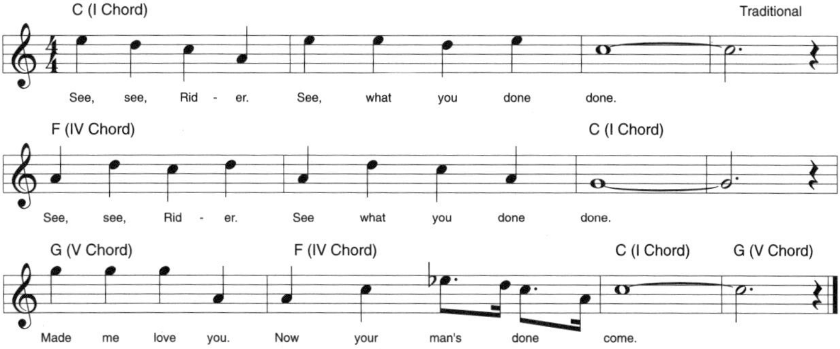

Take away the words and melody notes, and you have the chord structure for any basic 12-bar blues in the key of C, as shown in the following diagram.

Basic Blues

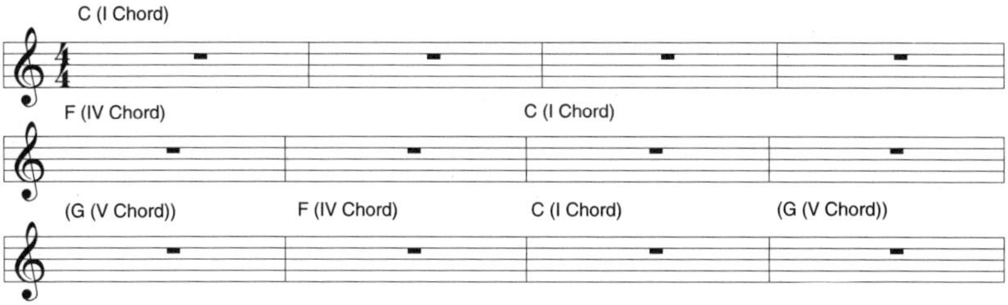

However, to keep things as simple as possible at first, you want to learn an even more stripped down version. So, for novices, we simplify the last line by taking out the IV Chord and the V Chord turnaround at the end. You'll still hear them on the CD so you recognize the turnaround, but what you'll play is this:

Easiest Basic Blues

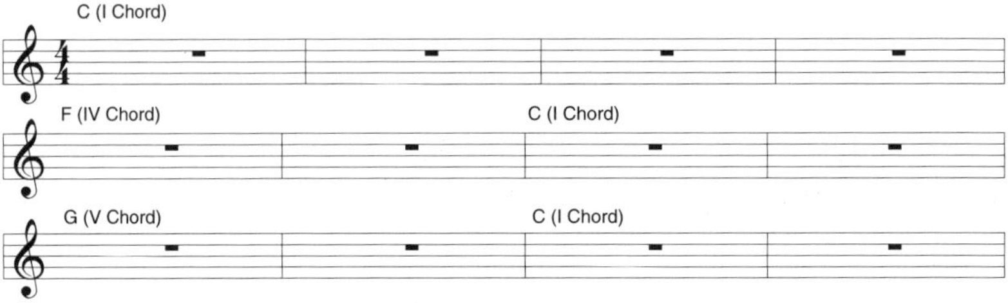

You can use these chords to play any 12-bar blues in C, including your lesson tune, *Blue Monk*.

Now, Bob tells you, it's time for the leap – to see how all this esoteric knowledge fits into real, living, breathing music. He puts on the Garage Band CD and asks you to just listen, counting off the bars of the C blues as they play. He wants you to follow the form on the written page and point to the chord that's being played, moving from one to another along with the music.

The CD starts up, and you hear the piano playing a chord that you assume to be a C (or I) chord. You point to it and, sure enough, Bob nods. After four bars, you hear a change in the piano, and you point to the F (or IV) chord. Bob nods again. After two more bars, you hear another change and point to the C. Again Bob nods. As the CD continues, you keep pointing and Bob keeps nodding. This is a snap, you realize. You have no trouble hearing the chord changes. Of course, it's not like all this is completely new. You've been playing along with the recorded rhythm section for more than a month now. You've heard these chords being played and have followed them by ear, intuitively. What Bob is doing is connecting the written chord symbols with the sounds you've been hearing, so you can understand the sounds better and use both the sounds and symbols to improve your music-making.

Now, Bob makes you play a slightly more difficult game. Instead of starting the CD at the beginning, he runs it forward to some place in the middle and tells you to listen again, figure out where the players are in the form and then point to the right chord.

When the CD starts, you have no idea where the players are. Of course, you panic, thinking you'll never be able to do this. A moment later, however, you are pleasantly surprised to hear what you realize is the ending of a chorus (which you recognize because it's the same bluesy turn-around sound you've heard all your life in rock, blues and jazz tunes: the rhythm section going to the V chord, then back to the I chord. The V chord is so distinctive even you couldn't miss it. When the turn-around is complete and the tune starts again, you point to the I Chord at the beginning and, sure enough, Bob nods. He stops the CD, runs it back a little and tries you again. The same thing happens. You're lost at first, but when the ending comes around, bang, you know it. He tries you again, and the same thing happens.

That's one of the beauties of basic blues, he says. It's hard to stay lost for more than 12 bars.

Now, you're ready to get back on the horn. Ultimately, you'll want to play riffs that center around chord tones and harmonize with them. At this point, of course, you know only one thing about each chord. You know the root note. The root note of the C chord is C. The root note of the F chord is F, etc. So, the first step is to simply play the root of each chord when the chord starts. So that's what Bob has you do. He starts the CD. The band leader counts off the tune: One and Two and One two three ... As the music begins, Bob points to the C chord and you play a C. The next bar, he points to the C again. You play another C. When the music gets to the F chord, he points and you play an F. And so forth.

When the musicians finish the form and start over, Bob goes back to the beginning and points to the C chord again, et cetera, et cetera, et cetera. After the second time through, he lets you do it by yourself, without the help of his pointing finger. No sweat.

You are now doing the same thing that any blues or jazz musician does when he or she improvises. You're playing notes that go along with the chord being played at that point. The only difference is that you're playing the simplest "riff" (one note) along with the most basic form of blues (few chord changes), where a jazz musician would be playing complicated riffs (lots of notes) along with a more complicated form (more chord changes). The principle is the same.

Trading Fours with a Little Structure

Anyway, after you click through this little exercise a few times, Bob says you're ready to play the blues again, utilizing all this new knowledge by staying within the chord structure as you and he trade fours.

You're a little doubtful, but Bob wags his finger at your doubt. All you have to do, he says, is start your four-bar solo on the root of the chord being played when you start your solo, then end on the root of the chord being played when you end your solo. In between, you can play any notes of the blues scale you want.

That sounds reasonable, but you still have doubts. When you look at the written form, however, you realize the task really is not so hard.

To solo on the first line, you start on a C and end on a C. To solo on the second four bars, you start on F and end on C. To solo on the third four bars, you start on a G and end on C.

Slightly impatient with your obvious self-doubt, Bob puts on the CD and tells you to get to work – which you do. You stumble a time or two, but for the most part you do exactly what he requested.

At this point, Bob shuts off the CD player, wipes the sweat from his brow and declares you've learned enough for one lesson.

Strangely enough, you're a little disappointed that he apparently has forgotten to harrass you about looking for a guitar playing partner, which is ironic since you actually have a little news to report on that front. Just as you're going out the door, however, he comes through.

"Oh, by the way, did you call Ben?"

You're ebullient. "I did. He gave me a couple of names."

"That's great. Did you set something up?"

"Not yet, but I'm going to."

"Yeah, right," Bob says. "Get out of here."

Here's what happened during Lesson 8

1. You learned that chords are named for the root note on which they're based.
2. You learned that musicians speak of the chord based on the first note of a scale as the I Chord; of the chord based on the second note as the II Chord; on the third as the III Chord, etc.
3. You learned that the three chords in a basic 12-bar blues progression are the I Chord, IV Chord and V Chord.
4. You learned that this 12-bar blues form is the same in hundreds of tunes.
5. You learned that the I Chord, IV Chord and V Chord in the key of C major are the C Chord, F Chord and G Chord.
6. You learned that lines of lyrics in 12-bar blues correspond to the four-bar phrases in the music.
7. You played along with the C blues tape and practiced starting and ending each four-bar phrase with the root note of the chord being played by the rhythm section.
8. Bob continued to nag you about finding a playing partner.

Lesson 9

By now, you're getting familiar enough with the Garage Band process to predict the hoops Bob will jump you through at the next lesson. When you show up for Lesson 9, he remains true to form. He starts you out playing along with the C blues CD. First you play the head, *Blue Monk*, then trade fours. Of course, Bob demands that you try to play the root of the appropriate chord at the beginning of each phrase, then improvise, which you can sort of do. When you finish, Bob notes that your tone has gotten better the last couple of weeks. Maybe, you respond, it's because you've been using that long-tone exercise to warm up every day.

Of course, Bob can't stand to let you rest on your laurels, so the next time you trade fours, he makes you play the root of the chord at the beginning of each bar (instead of each phrase), adding just a little more structure.

Once you hack your way through this second exercise with a minimum of stumbling, he announces it's time you learned the other notes of the chord to add to the root.

Picking up his horn, he plays what he tells you are the notes of a C major chord, going up the horn and then down again. When someone plays the tones of a chord that way, he says, it is called an arpeggio. He plays the sequence again and you realize it sounds vaguely familiar, conjuring up the fleeting image of a huge woman in a breast plate and horned helmet because it sounds the same as an opera singer exercising her voice before the show.

Bob plays the notes of the F major chord the same way. You comment that they sound just like the notes of the C major chord, only higher in pitch.

Good, Bob says, giving you a gold star. They sound that way because the notes of the F major chord have the same relationship to each other as the notes of a C major chord (or any other major chord for that matter). That's the idea. The notes of a major chord have a particular relationship to each other. When played together, they create a particular sound – a major sound.

He plays the notes of the C chord again, then tells you they are C, E, G, and then C again an octave higher. Then he has you play them along with him. Once you get that down, he tells you to pick out the notes of the F chord by ear. Just start on the F instead of the C, he says, then let your ear pick the other notes. You're doubtful at first, but find that after a few tries you soon identify the notes of the F chord. (They sound just like those of the C chord, only higher. Remember?) He has you do the same thing with the notes of the G chord, which you latch onto even more quickly.

You're doing great, he says. You've learned your three chords in the key of C the way you ought to – by ear. If you're interested, of course, you may want to look at your written scales to better understand the relationships of the notes in the chord.

Since you are curious (and want your money's worth from these lessons) you ask him to explain now. He tells you to look at the C major scale, as shown in the following diagram.

The notes of the C major chord, he reminds you, are C, E and G. If you look at the written scale, you will discover C, E and G are the first, third and fifth notes of the C major scale. That's their relationship and the way to identify the notes in any major chord. The notes of the major chord are always the first, third and fifth notes of the major scale, beginning with the root of the chord.

C Major Scale

You're not feeling so quick today, so you have him write out the F major scale, too.

F Major Scale

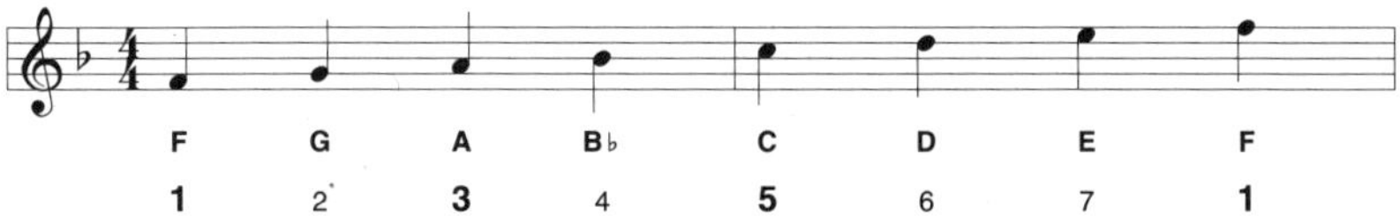

Then you can see it. The notes of the F chord are the first, third and fifth notes of the F major scale – F, A and C. Sure enough, F, A, and C were the notes you picked out when you played the F chord by ear.

Just to set this concept in concrete, you have Bob write out the G major scale, too.

G Major Scale

Yes, you see, the first third and fifth notes are the G, B and D, the same notes you picked out by ear.

Now, he says, you know enough to learn what he considers the best and quickest method for making a tune like *Blue Monk* a permanent part of your repertoire. It involves four steps.

- The first is to learn the melody, which you've done.
- The second is to go through the form, playing the root of the chord at the beginning of each phrase – which you've done.
- The third – coming up – is to "arpeggiate" the chords.
- The fourth, which you can try at home this week, is to include little pieces of the melody in your improvised solo.

Before you have time to ask, Bob explains that the verb arpeggiate is taken from the noun arpeggio, which just means the notes of a chord played one at a time in order. To arpeggiate simply means to play the notes of an arpeggio (like an opera singer does when she's warming up her voice before the show). When Bob finishes talking, you and he try this together a few times, playing:

- The **C E G C** of the C chord;
- The **F A C F** of the F chord; and
- The **G B D G** of the G chord.

Then he puts on the CD and announces that you're ready to trade fours again, arpeggiating with the music this time. Surprisingly enough, you accomplish this feat with only a few missteps. When you arpeggiate, you play slowly, of course, one note per beat, so the arpeggios sound square and blocky, not bluesy at all. When Bob plays his fours, however, he doesn't sound blocky. His solos swing, which makes you suspicious that he's throwing in some extra notes. You quiz him on that, but he shakes his head. They were all major chord arpeggios, he says. Once you get them under your fingers, you can make them swing, too.

Just to show you what's possible, he picks up his horn again and rips through the form a couple of times at breakneck speed, all over the horn. You laugh and shake your head as he plays. That can't just be arpeggios, you say. Yep, he says, just reorganized and rhythmically refitted, another tool in your musical rollaway. Get the arpeggios under your fingers, and you can do it, too.

With that encouragement, he sends you home with orders to practice all four steps in making *Blue Monk* your own. He doesn't say a word about whether you had called those guitar students, which strikes fear in your heart that maybe he's given up on ever getting you to play with someone else, which you know you'll do if you can just get up your nerve and the free time at the same moment.

1. Bob listened to what you'd practiced all week (and would have suggested corrections if any had been necessary).
2. You learned the notes of the I, IV and V major chords in the key of C.
3. You learned how major chords are constructed.
4. You learned that a good way to take possession of a tune involves four steps:
   a. Get the head (melody) under your fingers.
   b. Go through the form, playing the root of each chord as it comes up.
   c. Go through the form, arpeggiating each chord as it comes up.
   d. Slip pieces of the melody into your improvised solos.
5. You learned what arpeggiating means.
6. You tried arpeggiating the chords along with the C blues recording
7. You gave yourself a good kicking for not yet going after a playing partner, even though Bob failed to bring up this uncomfortable topic.

Here's what happened during Lesson 9

7

GARAGE BAND BASICS Part 4

The next night when you amble out to the garage to practice, you make an interesting discovery. Your garage is starting to look more like a music room than a home for your Mazda. In fact, you've started parking the car in the driveway, so you don't have to move your music stand out of the way every day.

Jane, it turns out, bought the music stand for you at a yard sale. You told her you didn't read music yet, but she said the stand was so cheap she couldn't resist. (Besides, your playing sounds so good from inside the house, she can't really believe you don't read music.) Since she brought the music stand home, you've actually been trying to read a little on your own, working out pop tunes from a "fake" book you bought at your local music store. (A fake book is a big, fat book with a lot of songs in it. The songs usually include just a melody line, the chords and the words to one verse and the chorus. It's called a fake book because an accomplished improviser can look at what's there and "fake" the rest. In fact, that's what you've been doing, playing familiar tunes half by ear, half by reading. Fake books are fairly expensive – in the $20 to $40 range – but since they usually include 100 or more songs, they are by far the cheapest way to buy written tunes.)

Having nothing better to do one Saturday, you've also upgraded your sound system. Your old ghetto blaster was starting to rattle in one of the cones, so you took it down to Sam's Pawn and traded it and several ten-dollar bills for one of those big chrome jobs like the young brothers tote around in movies about the South Bronx. It has detachable speakers, which you've placed strategically at either end of the work bench. It also has twin mike inputs, one of them filled now by the plug on the end of a black cord that snakes out to the microphone and mike stand you picked up on sale at another music store, one filled with electric guitars, huge speakers and young people with frizzy hair.

You've discovered that taping your practice sessions really helps. In fact, you're rather proud of the way you patched your Sony Discman into the ghetto blaster so you can run the recorded rhythm section on the Discman while you play your horn through the mike, recording the whole kit and caboodle on the blaster – thus producing a tape of you playing along with the band. Amazingly enough, the results sound pretty good at times.

Last, but not least, you've dusted off and plugged in the little Sanyo refrigerator your Mom and Dad originally bought for your room at college. As in your college days, the fridge is full of ice cold root beer.

Playing with Other People

As usual, you start your practice session by popping yourself a brew and opening the garage door half way to admit air but keep out the neighbors' unwelcome stares. To warm up, you dutifully play your long tones on the C scale, but soon get tired of that and turn on the CD. Still being a good boy, you practice just like Bob said, playing the head to *Blue Monk* the first time through the form, then improvising, hitting the root of each chord. When you start the CD over, you try arpeggiating the chords (still pretty rough). Finally, you fashion solos around snippets of the melody (which you read from the written music).

By the time you run through the CD several more times and finish your first root beer, you're wondering whether you should make this a two-brew session. You want to play some more, but you're tired of discipline, hankering for a little fun. What the heck, you think. You pop the top off another bottle and have a couple of swigs while you switch the CD back to the G blues, figuring you'll play a little *Not Freddie*. You know it a lot better than *Blue Monk.*

Playing *Not Freddie* by memory along with the CD, you surprise yourself. You really do know this tune. Once you play the head a couple of times, you start improvising, just playing in the G blues scale, slow at first, doing whatever comes into your head, then building up momentum. Pretty soon, you're wailing, your eyes closed and heart thumping. By the time the CD ends, you're winded, feeling exceptionally pleased with yourself. That's when you open your eyes and see a frizzy-headed teen-age kid peering up under the garage door at you.

"That was cool," he says, grinning.

Embarrassed, but pleased, you thank him, not sure what to say. You don't realize this is the most important thing that's happened so far in your musical career.

The kid is embarrassed, too, but introduces himself and says he lives in the next block. His name's Mike, and he plays electric guitar. He and his girlfriend, who plays bass and sings, are learning some rock tunes. Maybe you'd like to come play with them some time.

Really? you say, half of you thinking this kid must be a terrible guitar player if he wants to play with you, the other half thinking you might have sounded pretty good from out on the sidewalk, the other half of you thinking, if this kid worked out you'd *never* have to call those guitar students.

Sure, he says. It would be fun.

Okay, you say. Sure, you'll think about it.

Great, he says, telling you which house he lives in and quickly making his escape because neither of you can think of anything else to say.

Lesson 10

When you show up at Bob's for your next lesson on Wednesday, you immediately tell him this story, amazed as you are, not to mention proud, that anybody thinks you play well enough to play with them. (Not to mention relieved that you apparently have been relieved of going out to track someone down.) Bob, of course, cuts to the chase and asks if you actually went over to the kid's house to play. Well, no, you say. Not yet. You want to practice some more first, you say, knowing this line is not going to get you anywhere with Bob.

Wrong, he says. The kid heard you play. If you're good enough for him, then you're good enough. You can all learn together. In fact, that's going to be your assignment for the week, to screw up your courage, go find the kid and discover what making music is all about. To help you, Bob says, he is going to vary from his lesson plan today, creating a new lesson on the spot, just for you.

First, however, he wants to hear you play *Blue Monk* and some C blues. When you've done that, he nods approvingly and says you can keep playing *Blue Monk* the same way for another week along with what he's going to teach you now about guitar players.

Mixing Horns and Guitar Players

The first thing you have to know about guitars, he says, is that when a guitarist plays the note you call a D, the guitarist calls it a C. When he plays what you call an E, he calls it a D. In other words, his name for the note will always be a whole step below your name for the note. The same thing goes for keys, of course. When the guitarist tells you he's playing the key of G, you'll play in what you call the key of A. If he's in A, you'll be in B.

You continue to look puzzled as Bob completes what he thinks is a perfectly clear explanation of this situation. So, he draws you a little chart like this:

Tenor Sax Key	A♭	A	B♭	B	C	C♯	D	E♭	E	F	F♯	G
Guitar Key	G♭	G	A♭	A	B♭	B	C	D♭	D	E♭	E	F

You can use this chart to transpose from any note on a guitar to the appropriate note on a tenor sax, he says. Don't worry about why you have to do this. The reasons have to do with acoustics, the design of musical instruments and the way notes show up on the written page, but they don't matter right now. Just accept the situation as one of those annoying little facts of life like neckties, office parties and people who talk too much.

All right. Now you know how to transpose the notes from the guitarist's key into the notes of your key. This will be a fairly simple job at first, Bob says, because you probably won't be playing melodies along with your guitarist friend. Rather, he'll play chords and you'll improvise on the blues scale. That's what rock is all about. So all you really need to know at first is the key and a vague idea of what chord is being played at any given moment.

When you prepare to play a song with your guitarist friends, just ask what key they'll be playing in. If they say G, then you know you play in A. Once you know that, just improvise on the A blues scale. Try to hit chord tones if you can, but once you get going, just use your ears and follow your intuition. Experiment. One of the nice things about playing with electric guitars is that they're really loud. That helps in two ways. At first, when you're experimenting, you can play softly and nobody but you will hear. Then, when you get onto what the guitarists are doing, you have to play loud to be heard. You have to be aggressive. That's good, too, because aggressiveness is a novice musician's best friend. Play with conviction, and many people will love you even if you're bad. Also, you get a better tone on the sax when you play with conviction.

That's great, you say, but Bob is forgetting one thing. You don't know how to play in the key of A. You've barely tasted the keys of G and C.

Good point, he says. The second most important thing to know about playing with rock and blues guitarists is that they almost always play in one of four keys – G, A, C and E. That's because of the way the strings of a guitar are tuned, which makes these four keys the easiest for guitarists to play.

So, Bob asks, if a guitarist plays in those keys, what keys will you play? Glancing back at the chart, you quickly see that G on the guitar transposes to A on the tenor sax; the key of A transposes to B; C to D; and E to F#. So the keys you'll be playing with your guitarist friends are A, B, D and F#.

This, of course, is where you once again tell Bob what you've been trying to bang into his head all along. You're not ready to play with these youngsters, because you obviously don't know how to play in A, B, D or F#.

Not to worry, Bob says. How long did it take you to start playing the C blues scale along with your C blues CD? One lesson, right? You learned the C blues scale, and fifteen minutes later you began noodling along with the recording. That's what you're going to do with your guitar pickers, only you're going to do it at their house, not Bob's.

To help you get started, Bob takes out a piece of staff paper and quickly writes down the major and blues scales in the keys of A, B, D and F#. That's all you need, he says. Go home, play them a few times, then find the guitar kid and get going.

What? you ask. Isn't he going to teach you these scales like he did the others?

Nope, he says. It's important that he go on with your lessons as planned, since he introduces new keys to you in a logical sequence. What you're talking about with the guitarists is extracurricular activity. This is your chance to realize your ultimate goal – playing music for fun with real live people. You are perfectly capable of learning the A, B, D and F# blues scales as you play with the guitarists. You won't pick up the scales all at once, of course. As the guitarists play, you'll work out riffs by ear using pieces of the scales – just like you've done along with the Garage Band Music CD.

Here's what happened during Lesson 10

1. You played *Blue Monk* and improvised on the C blues while Bob listened, then critiqued your performance.
2. You learned that when guitarists play the same note as a tenor sax, their written note is one whole step lower than the sax's written note.
3. You learned that "transpose" means to translate music from one key to another.
4. You learned that guitarists usually play in the keys of G, A, C or E, which means that a tenor sax accompanying them has to play in A, B, D or F#.
5. You learned that you already know enough to go out and play with other musicians.

The Crux of this Whole Matter

Now you face a dilemma. When you started taking sax lessons, you told Bob you wanted to play music with other people. And you meant it. Of course, when you started, the prospect of playing with other people lay off in the distant, hazy future, even when Bob nagged you about it – because the decision was ultimately up to you. Now, two months later, you're going to have to go knock on somebody's door, invite yourself in, put your sax together and play in front of strangers. Sure you can play at home in your own garage with a CD, but in front of somebody else? Along with them? What if you freeze up? What if you can't figure out the key they're playing? What if you squeak and squawk just because you're nervous?

Thinking these and other paranoid thoughts, you do what any normal American would do. You procrastinate. Every night, you go out to your garage and practice, feeling guilty because you're such a coward, hoping against hope that the kid will stop by again to encourage you, give you one more compliment that will boost your confidence just enough to get you down to his house that first time.

Of course, he never shows up, and you grow more anxious as the days pass, realizing you can't go to your next lesson and tell Bob you were too gutless to play with the kids. Finally, the evening before you're due to see Bob again, you do it. You drink a couple of root beers, practice a while, then stroll up the street toward the kid's house. You, of course, know which one it is since you've driven past and scoped it out several times.

Half a block away, you realize you can hear the booming of a bass guitar. When you get within a couple of houses, you can hear the lead guitar, too, and a female voice. They're obviously playing in the garage, doing a boogie that sounds a lot like ZZ Top. They've got the door halfway up, just like you do when you practice.

You feel immense relief at this realization. You'd feared you would have to knock on the door and risk talking to the kid's mother. Instead, you just do what the kid did at your house – peer under the garage door. Sure enough, there they are, complete with amplifiers and a Jimi Hendrix poster on the wall. The girl, who sports a Sinead O'Connor haircut, is singing through a mike. The volume, impressive, makes you hope that when you go home to get your sax you can also find the earplugs you bought the last time you went to a Grateful Dead concert. The kids sound good, though. Real good. Watching them, listening, you start thinking: You can do this. You can feel their groove.

Once they break and Mike introduces you to his girlfriend, Kelly, you head back to your house to get your horn, actually hurrying, thinking: You can do this.

A Comment on this Story and Finding Partners

Obviously, not everybody is going to fall into their first musical relationship this easily. Some of you are actually going to have to approach strangers and ask them if they'll try making music with you. Most of you, however, will find it surprisingly easy to find other players once you set your mind to it. There are tons of people in the world who can make music and would like to do it with other people, but are just too shy, lazy or short of time to seek partners. They're out there waiting for someone with the initiative to ask them. For more ideas on this essential topic, see the chapter on how to find musical friends.

Fulfillment

It turns out you can. When you return, the scenario runs pretty much as Bob predicted. When you ask if they know any 12-bar blues, they're not quite sure what a 12-bar blues is. They just learn tunes off the records, playing chords according to where the chords show up in the lyrics. They are, however, eager to learn. They listen attentively as you explain about the 12-bar form. At the same time, you are growing ever more confident as a result of their evident respect for your knowledge. These kids are nice. They're not going to care if you screw up. They're having fun. If you screw up, they'll just want to try again.

The kids are quick, too. They soon realize that one of their favorite songs, ZZ Top's *Back Door Love Affair*, is a 12-bar tune. You don't know the song, but figure you'll give it a try. (You're starting to feel a little cocky.) Besides, you know all 12-bar blues are basically the same. The kids are impressed with this obvious brashness.

Just as Bob predicted, they tell you they play *Back Door Love Affair* in G. Learning this fact, you consult the cheat sheet in your sax case and realize the key for your sax will be A. Stepping over into the corner, you warm up a little, picking out the A blues scale by ear, remembering it, getting it under your fingers as best you can.

When you're ready, Mike counts off the tempo and they crank into the tune. You listen once through the form, counting, shuffling your feet a little, feeling the groove in your body. The second time through, Kelly starts singing. Getting into it, you play some two-note fills during breaks in the lyrics, tentative at first, realizing what Bob said about the loudness of electric guitars is true. You can barely hear yourself.

The next time through, you blow louder, more confident because you know your fills worked the first time. This time, Mike and Kelly hear them, too. You can see the approval in their faces (and promptly feel a pleasurable surge of endorphins hit your brain).

After several verses, Kelly quits singing and Mike kicks into a solo. It sounds great, but you have a hard time listening because you realize that when he quits, you're going to have to play a solo, too – your first ever with other musicians. You think many thoughts – fear, pride, amazement, a wish that you'd drunk one more root beer – but mostly you listen to the bass, counting to keep your place in the tune and watching Mike's face to see if you can tell when he's going to quit.

Sure enough, after he's played through the form a couple of times and comes back into the turnaround, he looks over at you. You're on. Completely paralyzed, unable to think of anything so rational as how your fingers play the A blues scale, you reach for any straw you can find. You come up with one thing. You remember the two notes of the fill you played while Kelly was singing. So you play these two notes: pah doooo-OOOOOO-ooooooo, pah dooo Pah dooo, pah doooo-OOOOOO-ooooooo, blowing as hard as you can to be heard over the guitars, trying to remember what Bob said about following your ear. Amazingly, you sound good. Then you actually do hear the guitars change chords. You follow by ear (since you can't remember the IV chord in A), adding a higher note to your riff. When they slip back to the I chord, so do you. Finally, at the turnaround, you follow again, adding one more higher and very blue note to your licks.

Starting into the form the second time, you realize you now know four notes that sound good in this tune. Thus armed, you relax, closing your eyes, grooving with the rhythm now, playing those four notes in whatever sequence they come into your fingers, listening to the guitars and following, blowing hard, really wailing by the time you swing into the turnaround and decide you'd better taper off, opening your eyes to see what the kids think. As you fade out, you find clear-cut approval in their shining faces.

Kelly grins and bangs into the words of the next verse.

Relieved to be done, you kick back, listening to her and savoring an indescribably delicious glow at having played a successful solo with actual musicians. This, you realize, is fun of a higher order. At last, you understand why Bob nagged you so much about this. You also remember his prediction that once you reach this point, you'll never look back. You'll always be a musician. Is that possible? you wonder.

Lesson 11

The next evening at Bob's, you can't wait to tell him what happened. As you relate the most salient details of your experience (trying not to sound too much like a kid raving to his dad), Bob gets a self-satisfied look on his face. When you're done, he smiles and says, "I told you." Over the next 10 minutes, he asks you questions about your jam, letting you revel in your triumph. Did they play 12-bar tunes? Could you follow the chord changes? Were you able to hit chord tones? How'd the kids like what you did? Did you teach them *Blue Monk* and *Freddie*?

When he decides you've had enough exultation, he makes you sit down and play your C blues along with the CD, arpeggiating the chords. The results are a little rough, considering you're now a rising star on the local music scene, but Bob just nods and says you've got a pretty fair grasp of C blues. Next week, he'll start you on the key of F major. At home this week he wants you to work on a little problem with your tonguing. (He's been meaning to bring this up for a couple of weeks and figures this is a good time since your ego is particularly robust today.) The rest of the lesson, you work on the tonguing exercise that he says will help you learn how to articulate each note the way you want, giving it punch when you want punch and slur when you want slur.

Here's what happened during Lesson 11

1. Bob talked to you at length about your first jam, letting you savor the memory and raising questions to help you think about various aspects of what you had done.
2. Bob listened to you play your C blues and decided you're ready to go on to your next key – F major.
3. Bob decided you were ready to work on your tonguing and gave you an articulation exercise to help improve it.

The Rest of the Lessons

We could go on and write a narrative for each of the 40 or so remaining lessons it would take you – our "typical" student – to work through the Garage Band basics. We won't, though, because the process now becomes increasingly repetitive. You've seen enough to understand how all this works. That's what you need for the present. In the following chapters, we will tell you how to apply this understanding to your own situation. Right now, when you've just seen how a novice can start playing fun music with other people after just a couple of months of lessons, is a good time to accelerate the discussion. Playing with other people is the point at which a person is truly hooked and will do whatever it takes to get better.

From here on out, the lessons are basically the same. Only the keys change. Every four weeks or so, you will learn a new one. Each week, you will practice at home along with your rhythm-section recording. You will begin each lesson by playing what you practiced during the week, sometimes with the teacher, sometimes along with the CD, sometimes by yourself. No matter how you do it, the teacher listens and evaluates. Much of the time, he will simply say you're doing fine (or great). He will always, however, be watching the basic elements of your playing, which for the sax are:

- **Tone:** The quality of the sound coming out of the horn, whether it is fat and full of emotion or thin and lifeless.
- **Embouchure:** The way the player's lips fit around and hold the mouthpiece.
- **Technique:** The way a player moves from note to note and makes them sound them sound the way he or she wants them to sound when they come out.
- **Breath support:** The control of the airstream through the horn.
- **Dynamics:** The increase and decrease of volume in a tune to create different moods.
- **Articulation:** The way a player separates notes, e.g., by slurring from one to another or tick ticking them out in a staccato way, etc.

Whenever he sees an opportunity to improve your playing by having you focus on one of these elements, he will give you a new and appropriate exercise. These are exercises you would be doing day by day, week by week under a traditional method. The difference in the Garage Band approach is that the teacher will never give you an assignment designed to help you somewhere in the distant, hazy future. Rather, he or she will emphasize instant gratification, providing advice that will make you a better player within the next few days or weeks.

The Other Keys

As we said, the remaining lessons are built around the 10 remaining major keys, which will be addressed more or less as follows in Lessons

Sharps and Flats Reminder

In case you've forgotten since we mentioned it the last time, a flatted note is a half step lower than the original note, a sharped note is a half step higher.

11-50: F major, D major, B♭ major, A major, E♭ major, E major, A♭ major, B major, C♯ major and F♯ major. You will learn the same basic elements in each of these keys that you learned in the keys of G major and C major: the major and blues scales, a 12-bar blues head and the I, IV and V chords in the key.

A Little About Practice

As we said, the schedule above is for you, our typical student. Some people will move more quickly, others more slowly. The most important ingredient in how quickly one advances is practice. **Anyone** who plays a half hour or more a day will move along at more or less the rate described here. You are much better off to play your instrument for even 15 or 20 minutes each day than to play for two hours twice a week. Pianist Arthur Rubenstein once said, "If I don't practice one day, I know it. If I don't practice two days, my friends and family know it. If I don't practice three days, the whole world knows it." As we've said before, music is an athletic endeavor. In most sports, you use your big muscles and control them with your eyes. In music, you use small muscles and control them with your ears. The principle is the same. You have to condition your muscles and train the sensory controller little by little each day. That's why the Garage Band approach works, because it makes you want to practice.

Concepts Covered in the Remaining Lessons

As you progress through the remaining lessons and keys, you will learn additional concepts. Unfortunately, we can't tell you exactly when your teacher will or should introduce these concepts. One of the most important rules of the Garage Band approach is that you not be forced to deal with new information until you need it. Making the decision about when to address the following topics is the teacher's job. The goal is to provide you with each new tool at the precise moment the tool will help you surge forward in a leap of improved playing.

The topics are:

- **Major Blues**: So far, you have been playing straight blues – which give you a hard, traditional blues sound like that of most electric blues bands. You obtain this straight blues sound using the blues scale of the key in which you are improvising. Later, you will learn that you can obtain a lighter, jazzier blues sound by using the blues scale from the related minor key. In the key of C major, for example, you'll use the A blues scale. In G, you'll use the E blues scale. In F major, the D blues scale, et cetera. We call this concept major blues. It will increase your improvising power 100 percent.
- **Ballads and Different Chord Progressions**: As you become a better player, you'll want to expand your horizons beyond the 12-bar blues. As we've said before, the basic difference between you as a novice and Branford Marsalis as a virtuoso is that you play simple riffs on simple chord progressions, whereas Branford plays complex riffs on complex chord progressions. Your next baby step toward Marsalisdom will be from playing 12-bar blues to playing

ballads (a ballad is just a slow tune) with slightly more complicated chord progressions.

- **Other Scales:** In addition to learning how to play the blues scale from one key over a chord progression in another key, you will also learn to solo using two other scales, the dorian and dominant. (These scales, you may recall, are included in your musical tool kits.) Each of these scales will allow you to create yet another sound as you solo.
- **A Vocabulary of Riffs**: When you speak, you don't make up your words as you go along. You combine the words you know into new thoughts. Improvising musicians do the same thing, but instead of words they use riffs. As you progress, your teacher will hound you to keep learning new riffs, building up your musical vocabulary. He'll teach you to lift riffs from many sources – from him, from records, from fellow players, from written songs and from anywhere else you can find them.
- **Solo Shaping**: Good musical solos are not mere series of notes strung together to show off the technical expertise of the player. They are emotional and intellectual statements. To add emotional and intellectual color to your playing requires that you knead and shape the string of notes you play. For example, one common way to shape a solo is to start out playing softly, grow gradually louder until the solo peaks at the proper moment, then taper off. Another way is to start off playing few notes per bar, gradually increasing and decreasing the stream of notes as the mood demands.
- **Vertical Soloing**: So far, you have been doing what is known as "linear" soloing. Linear simply means "in a line." That's how you've been using the notes of the blues scale, playing them one after another as your ear chooses. Eventually, Bob will teach you about vertical soloing, which relies more upon the notes of the

chord being played by the rhythm section and less upon any particular scale. (The "vertical" name comes from the fact that the written notes of a chord are usually stacked one upon another as shown below. When you solo vertically, you move vertically, up and down the stack, playing the notes of the chord in various ways.) This concept will increase your soloing power another 100 percent.

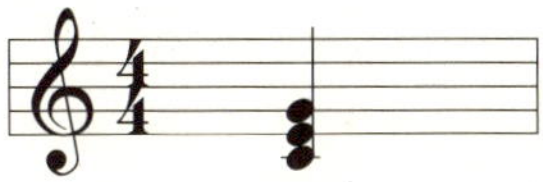

C Major
Chord

G **Fifth**

E **Major Third**

C **Root**

Vertical Soloing

When you solo using the notes of the chord, it is called "vertical" soloing because the notes of a chord are stacked on top of each other when written in a score.

- **Learning the Same Tune in Different Keys**: The more you play with other people, the more you'll want to know how to play each tune in more than one key. Sometimes you'll have to do it because the other players know the song in only one key. Other times you'll be playing with a singer whose voice has a range that limits him or her to certain keys on certain songs. Also, learning a familiar tune in a new key is a good way to become more comfortable with your instrument.
- **Minor Chords and Keys**: Before you go too far, you need to learn how to create the mysterious sound of such tunes as House of the Rising Sun and St. James Infirmary by using minor chords and playing in minor keys. (For those of you who are just naturally

curious, a minor chord is one in which the major third has been lowered a half step to what is known as the minor third. When a tune is in a minor key, that simply means it is built primarily upon minor chords.)

- **Vibrato**: As you compare your early saxophone playing to that of more accomplished musicians, you'll find one of your biggest deficiencies is an almost indefinable quality we call touch. Where the more experienced player sounds warm, woozy and sensitive, you sound square and blocky. A large part of the warmth you seek will come from something called vibrato, which (at its most obvious) is the sound a player makes when he or she holds a long tone and makes it quaver with a golden wahwahwahwahwahwahwahwahwahhhhhhhhh.
- **Reading Music**: As you become a better player, you most likely will want to learn to really read music. For one thing, reading will let you play arranged music along with other musicians, which can be a lot of fun. For another, reading opens the door to thousands of tunes you may not learn except from a book.
- **Solo transcriptions**: One of the great resources for improvisers is transcriptions of recorded solos by great players. We owe a great debt to transcribers who sit down with a recording, their instrument and staff paper to painstakingly reduce the recorded music of a Charlie Parker or Eric Clapton to marks on a page. With your teacher's help, you will read and play the solos of the masters not so you can play the music exactly as they did or do, but so you can learn how they make rhythms and harmonies work in their music.

SUMMARY OF THE GARAGE BAND BASICS

We thought it might be nice to summarize the lessons again to help you remember how the basics fit together. The kind of teacher we describe in our chapter on finding a teacher should be able to use this recapitulation as a guide for devising his or her own lessons.

Lessons 1-6 (more or less)

(This can take place over a period of four to six weeks, depending on the student.)

1. Learn the G blues scale and G major scale.
2. Learn that keeping the rhythm of the groove is the most important thing for a beginning musician.
3. Learn to groove along with a recorded rhythm section playing 12-bar blues in G by using random notes from the G blues scale.
4. Learn a 12-bar blues melody in G by ear. Also learn to read the notes on a page, just to help you remember the tune.

Lessons 7-13 (more or less)

1. Move to the key of C, repeating the process you went through for the key of G, i.e., learn the C blues and major scales and to groove along with a C blues using random notes from the C blues scale.
2. Learn how major chords are spelled.
3. Learn about the I, IV and V chords, how they get their names and that they're the three chords used in basic 12-bar blues.
4. Learn the I, IV and V chords for the key of C and how they fall in the chord progression.
5. Add some structure to your improvising along with the C blues by

SUMMARY, continued . . .

beginning and ending each four-bar phrase with the root note of the chord being played.

6. Learn a 12-bar blues melody in C.

The Rest of the Lessons

From here on out, the lessons are basically the same. Only the keys change. Every four weeks or so you learn a new one, practicing at home along with your rhythm- section recording. As you proceed through each key, the teacher will listen and coach you on the basic elements, which for the sax are:

— Tone
— Embouchure
— Technique
— Breath support
— Dynamics
— Articulation

In addition, the teacher will introduce the following concepts and tools, one at a time, as you are ready to use them to improve your playing:

— Major Blues
— Ballads and Different Chord Progressions
— Other Scales
— A Vocabulary of Riffs
— Solo Shaping
— Vertical Soloing
— Minor Chords and Keys
— Learning the Same Tune in Different Keys
— Vibrato
— Reading Music
— Solo Transcriptions

If you practice 20 minutes or more every day, this whole process will take about four weeks for each of the 12 keys. You can be playing music and having fun after the first two to five weeks. The more you practice, the faster it will go.

The Result

After you have gone through this process for all 12 keys, you will:

— Have a basic mastery of the instrument.
— Know your blues scales, major scales and major chords in all 12 keys.
— Be able to jam with anybody playing blues in any key.
— Be poised to progress as far as you want in music because you will know how to learn whatever you want.

8

TRANSLATING WHAT YOU'VE LEARNED TO THE GUITAR

In the last three chapters, we described how the Garage Band method works for one instrument – the tenor sax. In this and successive chapters, we'll describe how to apply the fundamentals to other instruments.

It's All in the Groove

As we've said before, the secret of the Garage Band approach for any instrument is to:

- Start by learning a simple, fun way to groove along with 12-bar blues.
- Move through a step-by-step process that maintains the fun of playing and leads to a genuine command of the instrument.

The process is pretty much the same for all instruments. The "simple way to groove" is different, however, because some instruments can play more than one note at a time.

Our Guitar Man

We wrote this section on playing the guitar with the help of our jazz, rock and blues guitarist friend Ben Burdick. Ben uses the method with his students at Old Boise Music. He's been a working musician since age 16.

Ben Burdick

Guitar's Fret Board

The diagram at right shows how you change notes on a guitar by moving from fret to fret. When you move from one fret to another along the same string, you shorten the string enough to raise the tone by one half step.

A Note On Sharps and Flats

For those of you who don't know: a D♯ is a half tone higher than a D; an E♭ is a half tone lower than an E. So a D♯ is the same note as an E♭.

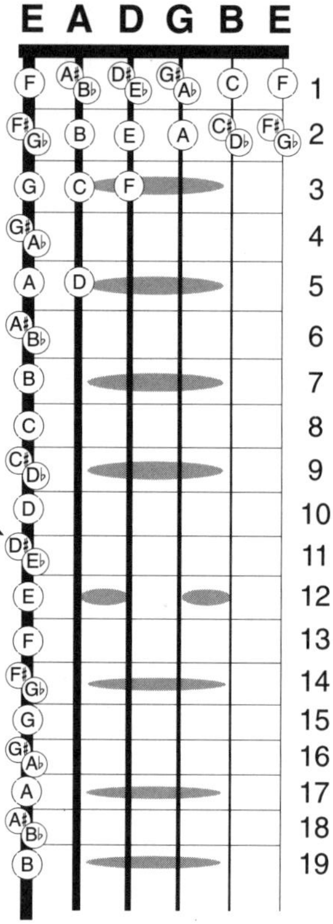

The User-Friendly Electric Guitar

When people in America talk about guitars, they're really talking about three different classes of instruments:

- The acoustic classical guitar – which has nylon strings and a wide neck. As the name implies, it is played primarily by those who pick classical tunes and cherish this instrument's sweet sound.
- The acoustic steel-string or flat-top guitar – which may have a wide or narrow neck, depending on the philosophy of the guitar maker. It has a twangier, down-home sound.
- The electric guitar – which has lighter gauge steel strings than the acoustic flat-top, has a narrow neck and comes with a magnetic pick-up built into the body to transmit the vibration of the strings to an amplifier.

Generally speaking, anything that can be done with a guitar can be done more easily with an electric – primarily because you need less strength and endurance to press the strings against the frets on the neck. (Frets are the thin strips of metal inlaid across the guitar's neck at precise intervals. When you press a string against a fret, you shorten the playing length of the string and raise the tone.)

Fretting an electric guitar is easier because the strings of an electric are closer to the fret board and are of a lighter gauge than the strings of an acoustic. (The strings on an acoustic guitar have to be bigger and must vibrate a greater distance to create their own sound.)

Why We Focus on the Electric Guitar

The electric guitar's user friendliness is the main reason we focus our discussion of the guitar on the electric version. We're trying to get you into playing American music the easiest, quickest way possible.

The electric guitar fills the bill for that task – even if you don't want to be a noisy, obnoxious rocker. Think of the electric guitar as a step toward what you really want to do. Also remember that you can buy an electric guitar that will produce almost any quality of sound you want. With a big, hollow-body electric you can get a sweet acoustic sound, even a classical sound. If you want to play an acoustic later, plan on it. But if you want to learn as quickly as possible – and become as proficient as you can – start on an electric.

The second reason we focus on the electric is that nowadays the electric guitar is the guitar of choice for making the genre of music employed as a learning tool in the Garage Band method – 12-bar blues. The third is that to play along with any instruments besides an acoustic guitar, you need an electric so you can be heard (and hear yourself).

Henceforth, when we use the word guitar, we will be talking about electric guitars. If you want to start with an acoustic because of its sound and mobility, more power to you. This stuff all applies to acoustic guitars; learning some things will just be physically more demanding with an acoustic.

The Guitar Has Two Functions

As a novice guitar player, you'll start out exactly as the saxophone player did. You begin by learning to groove in a simple way, playing hip music. The major difference is that the guitar has two functions, so you have to learn two ways to groove. The saxophone functions primarily as a solo or melody instrument. Obviously, you can play a guitar the same way – soloing one note at a time. That's the first of the guitar's functions. However, you also can play more than one note at a time on a guitar. This allows the guitar to perform another function, that of a rhythm instrument striking chords and keeping the groove of a tune going while other instruments and voices solo.

The Garage Band Approach for Soloing on Guitar

Since the guitar has two musical functions, the approach to learning the guitar follows two simultaneous tracks, one for soloing and one for playing rhythm. We start with the solo track because it's easier and is similar to that used when learning to play the saxophone.

Our Garage Band sax student started learning to play the sax by learning to finger and play the notes of a blues scale in one key, then using a couple of those notes to groove along with a recorded rhythm section. Once the student could groove in the first key, he went on to learn another key and another and another. As the student worked through the scales in different keys, he gradually became more adept at all aspects of the sax. Along the way, he picked up various elements of playing as he became able to use them. After 12 months or so, this average sax student could improvise over all 12 keys. You do the same things as you learn to solo on the guitar, only faster.

You Can Learn to Solo in the Key of A in 20 Minutes

To make things as simple as possible, we start guitarists with an abbreviated four-note version of the blues scale instead of the full six-note scale learned by the saxophonist. This allows us to teach soloing with a visual tool that we call the rectangle system. It turns out that because of the geometric nature of the guitar neck, the four notes of our abbreviated blues scale lie in a rectangle, as shown in the following diagram for our rectangle in the key of A.

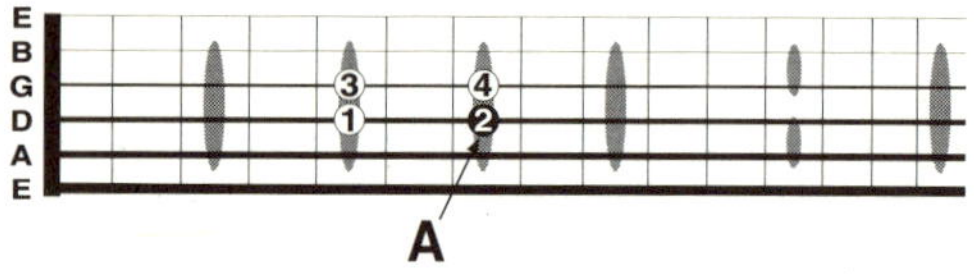

Rectangle in the Key of A
The four dots indicate the notes that can be used to play simple solos in the key of A. The black dot is an A, the root of the A chord.

Notes in this configuration are easy to play. If you finger the first note of the rectangle with your index finger, it's easy to move to the second note with your ring finger, then to the third with your index finger and the fourth with your ring finger as shown in the above illustrations.

You can start out improvising with these notes just as we did with the blues scale on the sax. Like the sax player, you'll first want to play call and response with the teacher to get the idea of what a riff sounds and feels like. The teacher will play a simple riff and you'll repeat it in rhythm. Then – as soon as you see how you can sound neat with just two or three notes – you can begin improvising along with a CD , just as the sax player did.

The key to success at this point is to keep your riffs simple and play them in time so they sound musical. Fight the temptation to learn complicated licks and phrases right off the bat. Anybody can learn a complicated lick demonstrated by a friend or teacher. All you have to do is play it over and over again. The hard part is fitting that lick into a tune and making it sound musical. What usually happens is that the novice gets a tune going, comes to the place where he wants to play that hard lick he's learned with such tedious dedication and *slows down* so he can fit in all those finger moves, which destroys the rhythm and beauty of the tune.

The more sensible approach is to start with just a few notes played gracefully. That's the whole idea of this endeavor – to make *music* from the start. That's what's fun. You can find lots of heros whose simplicity you can emulate from the beginning. Listen to guys like Albert Collins or B.B. King. You'll find some of their most hypnotic music is made up of two-, three- or four-note licks. At the start, copy those parts of their songs and focus on making them musical.

Of course, if you play your two-, three- or four-note licks all on the one rectangle we've described, you will get bored pretty quickly, even if you make them sound musical. Fortunately, you don't have to do that because the rectangle for the key of A repeats itself everywhere there is an A on the fret board. (See the diagram below.)

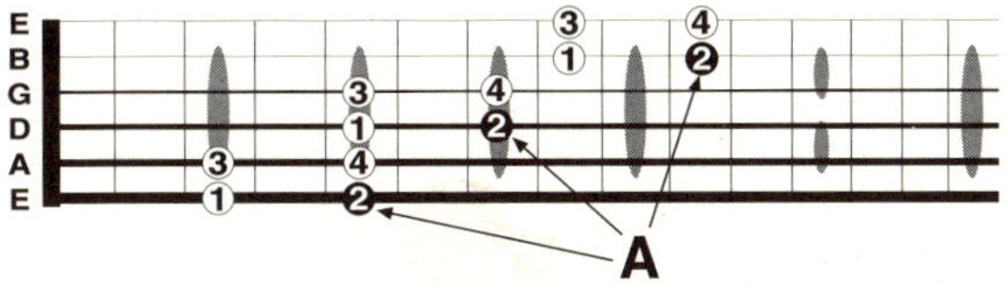

Three Rectangles in the Key of A
There is a rectangle for the key of A everywhere there is an A on the fretboard.

You can play the same licks on the four notes of each rectangle as you did on the first. They will sound the same, just higher or lower in pitch. That's because the notes of all the these rectangles are the same; they're just in different octaves.

You can learn all these rectangles in one lesson and be playing simple, but cool, solos in A in under 20 minutes *the same way that accomplished guitarists play,* which means you can steadily progress into more complex solos because you're doing it the right way.

You Can Do the Same Thing in Any Key

The nice thing about the guitar is that when you can solo in one key as described above, you can do it in any key. You can because the notes used to solo in other keys have the same relationship to each other as those in the key of A have to each other. They're simply a pattern. To change keys, all you have to do is move the pattern to a new starting point.

Here's how it works. If you look back at the previous diagrams, you'll see that for the key of A, the rectangles start with the ring finger on an A. Let's look at the key of B, which is a whole step higher than A. To play in the key of B, you pick up the rectangle (all in one piece) and move your ring finger to a B to play the rectangle there as shown in the following diagram:

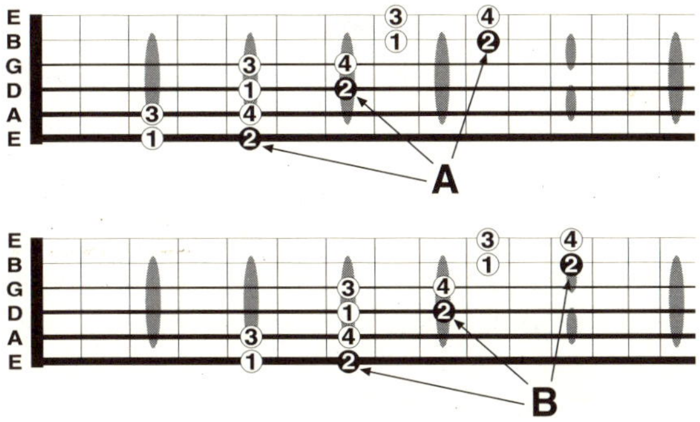

Three Rectangles in the Key of B

The dots in the diagram immediately above indicate the notes that can be used to play simple solos in the key of B. As you can see by comparison to the top diagram, the rectangles for B are just two frets (two musical half steps) higher than the rectangles for the key of A. That's because a B is two half steps higher than an A (A to B♭ to B)

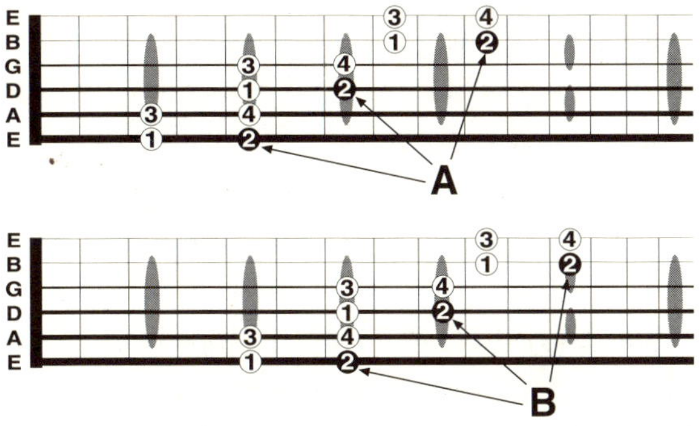

The Root Note is the "Home" Fret

You can find a rectangle for any key by putting your ring finger on the fret for the root note of the key (A for the key of A, B for the key of B, etc.) as indicated by the black dots in each of the rectangles in the diagrams.

To solo in F, you move the ring finger to an F. To play in G, you move the ring finger to the G. In other words, to play in any different key, you pick up the whole rectangle and move your ring finger to the root note of the key. Using this approach, most people can actually learn to solo in any key within a couple of months. You can't be Stevie Ray Vaughn that fast, but if you relax, keep things simple and focus on keeping time, you can play blues that sound the way blues are supposed to sound.

The Garage Band Approach for Playing Rhythm Guitar

Unfortunately, mastering everything we outlined in the section on soloing will not make you a rock and blues guitarist. When you join a band or accompany your own singing voice, you'll solo less than a fourth of the time. The rest of the time, you'll play rhythm. In a band, you'll be working with the drummer and bassist to maintain the form while other players solo. The good news is that playing rhythm guitar on blues and rock tunes is just as straightforward as learning to solo.

In earlier chapters, we described the chord structure of a tune as the skeleton on which the tune hangs. The rhythm players create and maintain that skeleton. At any given point in a tune, one or more of the rhythm players is striking a chord that gives the tune its "sound". In basic 12-bar blues and other simple music, the skeleton is made up of the three chords we described earlier in the book – the I Chord, the IV Chord and the V Chord of whatever key you're in. Playing rhythm guitar simply means keeping a groove going by strumming, thumping or otherwise striking each of those chords in the proper place in the proper rhythm at the proper tempo.

Learning to Play Chords an Easy Way

The first task for a rhythm player is to learn to finger the chords on the fret board. Since there are 12 tones and a chord for each tone (A♭, A, B♭, B, C, D♭, D, E♭, E, F, G♭, G), you might logically conclude you have to learn to finger a minimum of 12 chord patterns to play in all keys. That's a mistake a lot of novice guitarists make. This mistake is encouraged by many basic guitar books, which start off by teaching you what are known as "open" chords.

An open chord is one you finger at the very end of the fret board, so that you can strum not only the notes of the strings you're fretting, but also the "open" strings you're not fretting. This is an appealing way to start because the first open chords you learn are relatively easy to play and sound great – rich and full. It's also a trap. After you learn the first four or five open chords, the going starts getting rougher. As you work your way through the other open chords required to play in all keys, your fret hand and brain start overloading because every chord is different. You have too much information to process and too many moves to execute. You get frustrated.

With the open chord approach, you learn about some trees, but never get a look at the forest until you're way, way down the road. Most people quit learning before they get that far. They either give up the guitar or settle for playing a few common chords in the easiest keys. They never develop a command of the instrument. In the Garage Band approach, we start you with two-string patterns for the fret hand (for the I, IV and V chords) that will let you play these chords in any key by moving the finger patterns to different places on the fret board. Within a couple of lessons, you'll see the whole forest and all the trees.

The I, IV and V Chords in the Key of A

To get you started, we reduce the basic I, IV and V chords to their simplest, easiest-to-play form in the key of A. The chords are played on just two strings as illustrated in the diagram.

Simple I Chord in A (A chord)

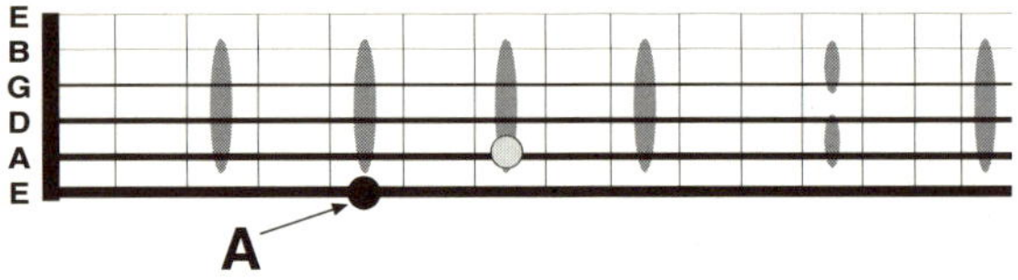

Simple IV Chord in A (D chord)

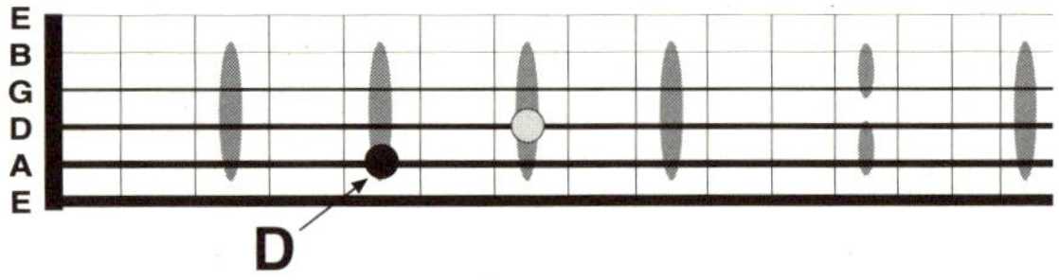

Simple V Chord in A (E chord)

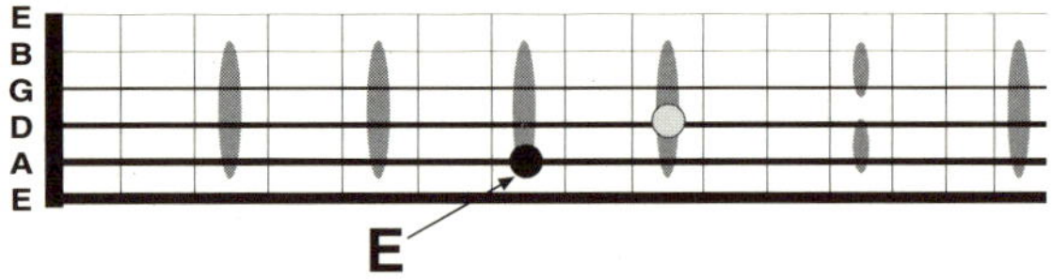

An Easy Way to Play Chords
The chords shown above are played with just two strings, but when played with different rhythms can sound great in hundreds of songs.

At the first lesson, you should learn how to finger these two-note chords with your left hand and strum the two strings with your right.

Different Rhythm, Different Song

As we said earlier, all basic 12-bar blues tunes are exactly the same in musical terms. The chord progression is always the same, just higher or lower depending on the key. Twelve-bar blues tunes sound different primarily because they have different words and/or different rhythms. For example, if you play *I've Got My Mojo Working* and Chuck Berry's *Memphis, Tennessee* in the key of A, you'll play the same chords in both songs. The songs sound different because *Memphis, Tennessee* has a different rhythm and different words.

Since you don't want all your songs to sound alike, the second step in the Garage Band approach for rhythm guitar is to equip yourself with a small, but versatile, repertoire of different, widely used rhythms. That's how we do it. At the first lesson, your teacher should demonstrate a version of the blues guitarist's most versatile and hard-used rhythm, the shuffle, which is the rhythm of tunes like *Sweet Home Chicago, I've Got My Mojo Working, (You Ain't Nothing But a) Hound Dog* and hundreds more. In the next several lessons, you'll want the teacher to show you how to play another standard version of the shuffle and two versions of what we call a straight or "rock" rhythm. (All these rhythms are illustrated on our play-along CD. They also are written out in guitar tablature in the appendices.) After three or four lessons, you'll be able to play 12-bar blues in the key of A with four different rhythms. You will be equipped to develop as large a repertoire of blues tunes as you want just as fast as you can learn the words, because these four rhythms are used in so many songs that we couldn't begin to count them. To recap, these rhythms are:

- A basic version of the shuffle. It's the one used by Stevie Ray Vaughan in the song *Boot Hill* on his *Sky is Crying* CD. The same version is used by Chuck Berry on *School Day* on his *Chess Box, Volume 1* CD.
- An alternative version of this basic shuffle, which often is associated with Jimmy Reed because Jimmy used it in so many of his songs. You'll find it in all the following songs on his *The Best of Jimmy Reed* CD: *Bright Lights, Big City; Down in Virginia; Going to New York; Baby What You Want Me to Do?; Aw Shucks Hush Your*

Mouth, and Laughing at the Blues.
- A basic Chuck-Berry-style rock rhythm, which Chuck used in *Oh Baby Doll* as reissued on the *Chess Box, Volume 1* CD (and a lot of other songs); and
- The alternative version of the Chuck-Berry-style rock rhythm, which Jimmy Reed used in two songs on the CD we mentioned a couple of paragraphs back, *The Best of Jimmy Reed.* Those songs are *Shame Shame Shame* and *I'm Going to Upside Your Head.*

In addition to playing these rhythms for you on our CD, we have written them out in musical notation and guitar tablature in the appendices, primarily so a teacher can look them up and see exactly which rhythm patterns we're talking about. We choose not to write them out in the text for a couple of reasons. For one thing, it's darn hard for a novice to decipher written rhythms and translate them to the guitar. Even if you can figure out how the rhythm is supposed to sound, it's hard to look at marks on a piece of paper and tell how you should hold and move the fingers of your *right* hand to strum the strings and make the sound you want. However, it is incredibly easy for a guitar-playing friend or teacher to show you these rhythms and how they're played. Any decent blues guitarist can teach you any one of these rhythms in less time than it takes to grill a hamburger. Your job is to get out of the house and find someone to show you what we've just described. You'll be way ahead for two reasons. One, you'll make a friend who's into music and, two, you'll learn quickly from a live human being instead of wasting hours agonizing over the hieroglyphics designed to communicate this stuff on paper.

Expanding into Another Key

If you wanted, you could be lazy and play in the key of A all your life. However, that would make it hard to play music with more energetic people who don't want to play in one key all the time. That's why, once you get comfortable with playing several rhythm in the key of A, you want to learn to play in other keys. That's when you want your teacher to take the next step, showing you how to use the same simple fingering patterns to play the I, IV and V chords for the key of B♭. They're illustrated in the diagram.

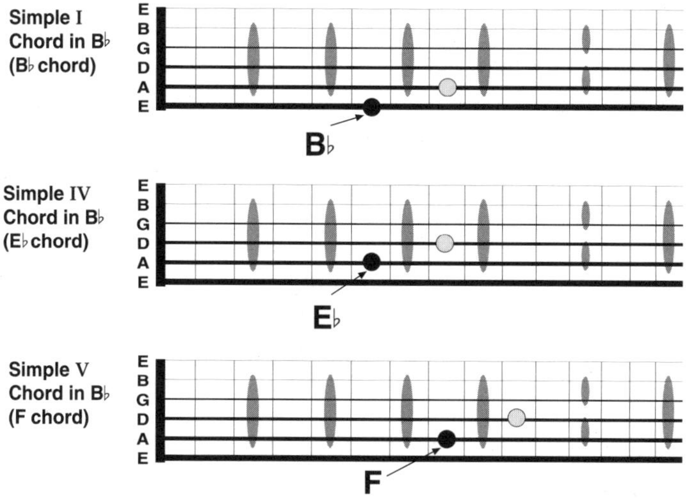

Chords for the Key of B♭
As you can see in the above diagram, the fingering patterns for the chords in B♭ are the same as those for the key of A, just one fret higher.

The patterns are the same basic "shapes" as the ones for the key of A. You just move them to different starting points. These are the patterns you'll use in all the keys.

Then You Can Play Rhythm in the Other Keys, Too

Once you get comfortable playing everything in the key of B♭ that you've played in A, which comes quickly, you can go on to chords shown in the next diagram, which illustrates how you can play in any key by moving the fingering patterns for the I, IV and V Chords to different positions on the fret board. That's all there is to it.

The way to find your starting place in each key is to remember that in each of these chords, your index finger will fret the root note of the chord. (Just as your ring finger uses the root note of the scale for home base when soloing on a rectangle as described earlier.)

As you learn how to play rhythm in this manner, you will be moving ahead on the solo track at a similar pace. So, when you reach the point where you can do what we've just described, you will be able to play 12-bar blues in any key with any band or recording. That shouldn't take more than a couple of months.

Simple I Chord in C (C chord)

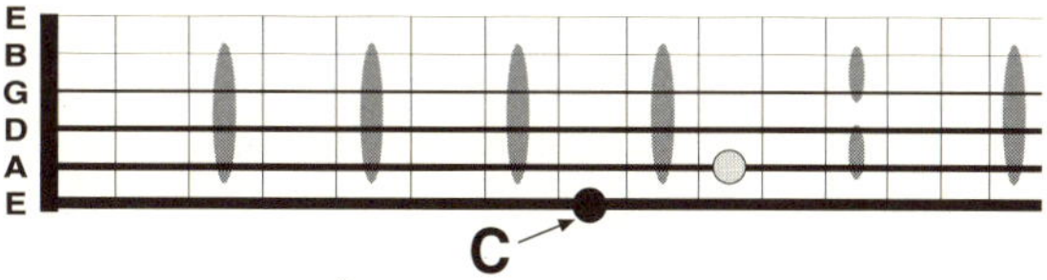

Simple IV Chord in C (F chord)

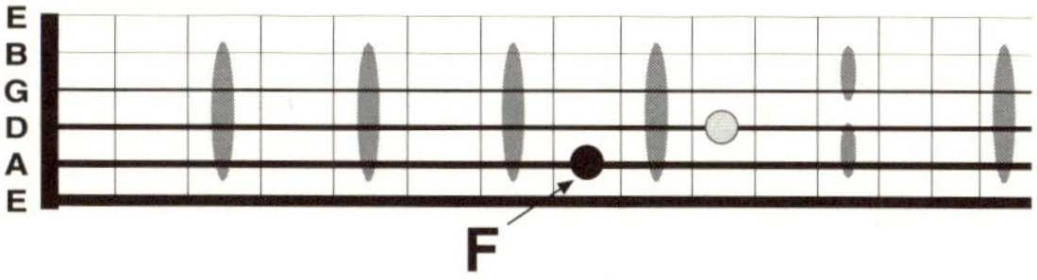

Simple V Chord in C (G chord)

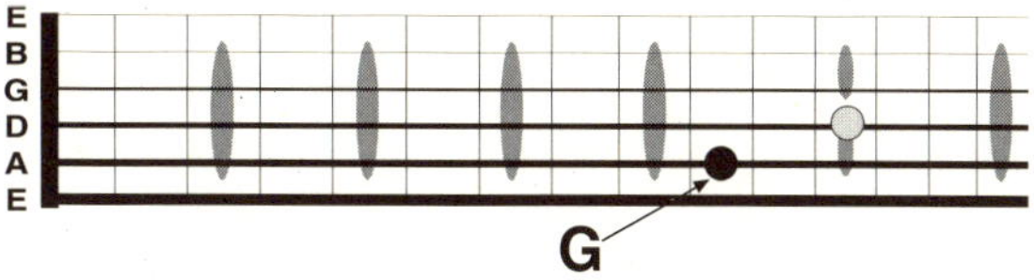

Chord for the Key of C

As you can see in the above diagram, the fingering patterns for the chords in C are the same as those for the key of B♭, just two frets higher. The next diagram shows the chords for the key of D, which once again are the same as for C and B♭, just a couple of frets higher. By continuing to move up the fret board, you can use these finger patterns to play in any key.

Simple I Chord in D (D chord)

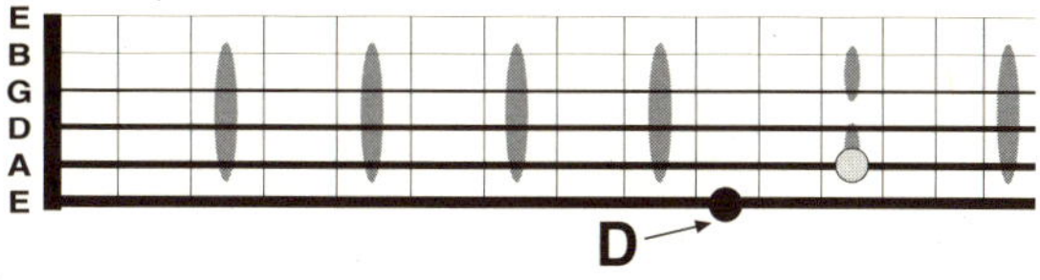

Simple IV Chord in D (G chord)

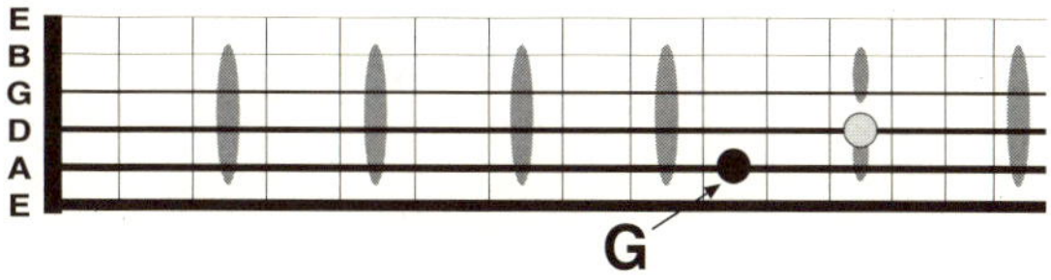

Simple V Chord in D (A chord)

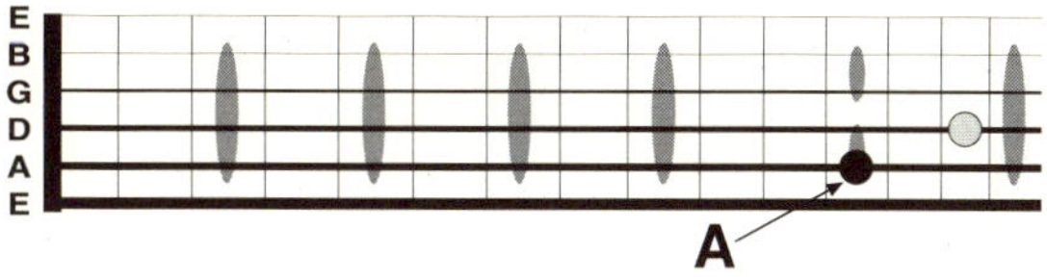

9

THE GUITAR
Part 2

Up to this point you will have been playing rhythm guitar using the simplest, easiest-to-play form of the I, IV and V chords. When you do the simplest, easiest-to-execute form of anything, you usually sacrifice something. That's true in this case, too. The chords we've discussed so far work and sound great, but are not as full-sounding and versatile as the ones usually played by accomplished guitarists. So, once you build up some strength and mobility in your fret hand, the next step will be to expand into what are known as barre chords – the ones usually used by accomplished players.

Learning to Play Barre Chords

As you will recall from the last diagram, you've been playing the I, IV and V chords for the key of D like this:

Simple I Chord in D (D chord)

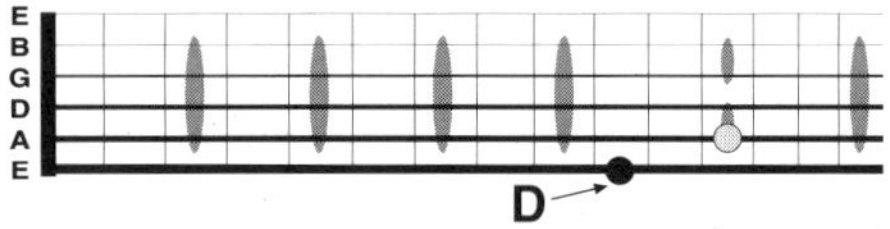

Simple IV Chord in D (G chord)

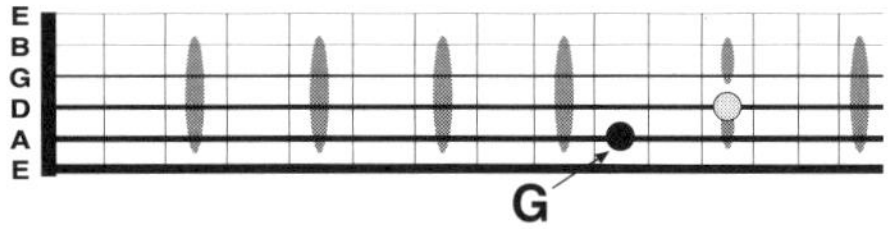

Simple V Chord in D (A chord)

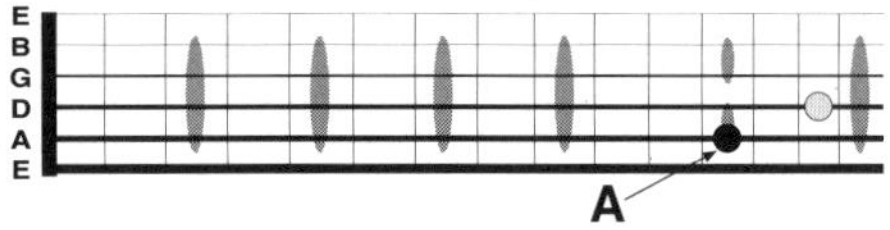

With the above fingerings, you play just two strings for a chord. In contrast, the I, IV and V **barre** chords in D are fingered like this, with the index finger holding down all the strings where the barre is shown:

Barred I Chord in D (D Chord)

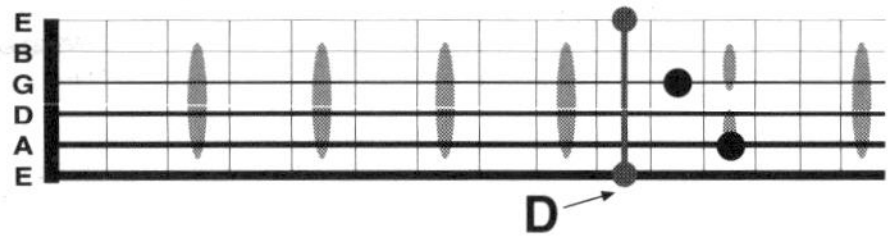

Barred IV Chord in D (G chord)

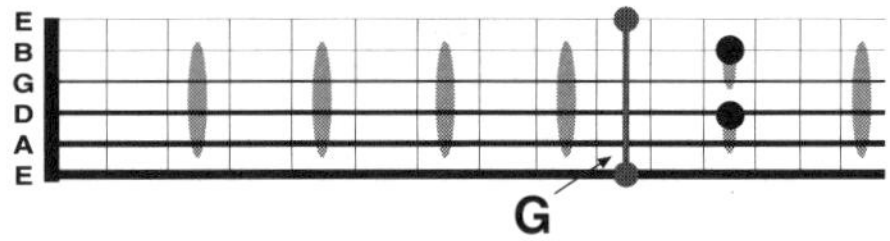

Barred V Chord in D (A chord)

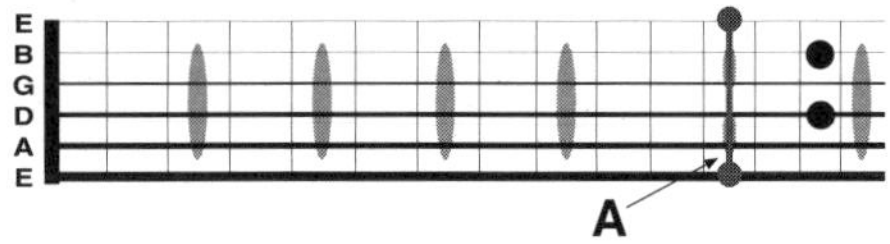

With the barre chord you can play all six strings, which gives you a much fuller sound. The following illustration shows how a barre chord is held, using the index finger as a "bar" (barre in guitarese).

Obviously, these chords require a firm grip on the fret board. They're a little bit hard on an acoustic guitar. They're way easier on an electric. That's the main reason we suggest you start out on an electric. Even on

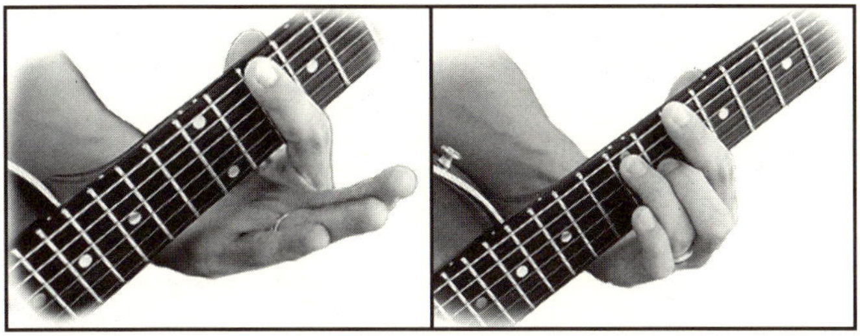

an electric, of course, you will need practice to develop a strong-enough grip for barre chords. Once you manage that grip, however, you will have reached cruising altitude for the Garage Band method for guitars, because you will be able to play the basic barre chords in any key simply by moving your fret hand to different positions as shown in the following diagrams.

Barred I
Chord in C
(C Chord)

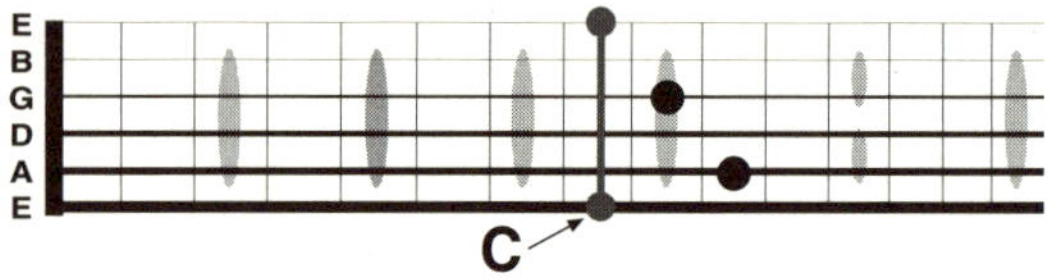

Barred IV
Chord in C
(F chord)

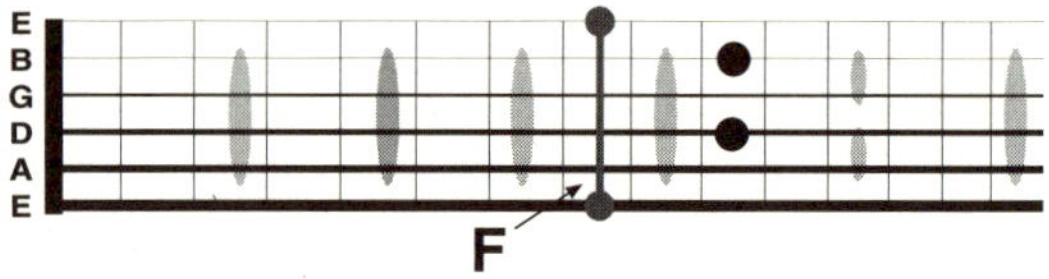

Barred V
Chord in C
(G chord)

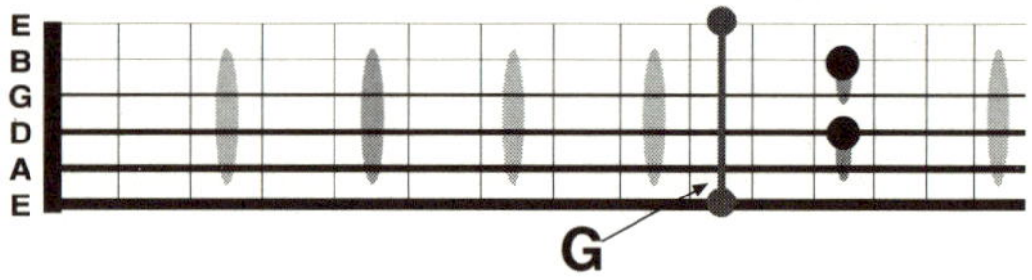

Barred Chords for the Key of C

The fingerings for the chords in C are the same as those in D. They've just been moved two frets because a C is two half steps lower than a D.

Barred I
Chord in A
(A Chord)

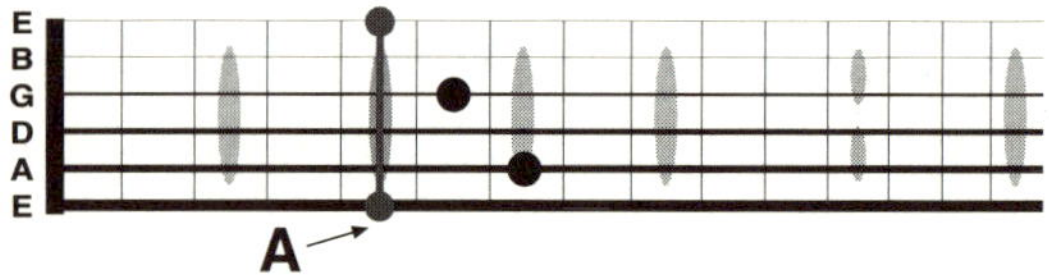

Barred IV
Chord in A
(D chord)

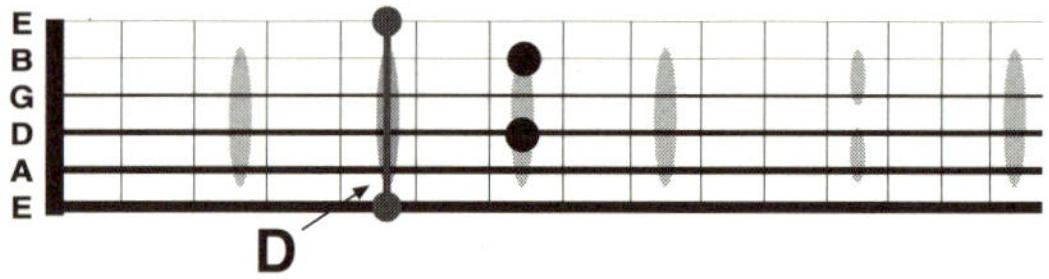

Barred V
Chord in A
(E chord)

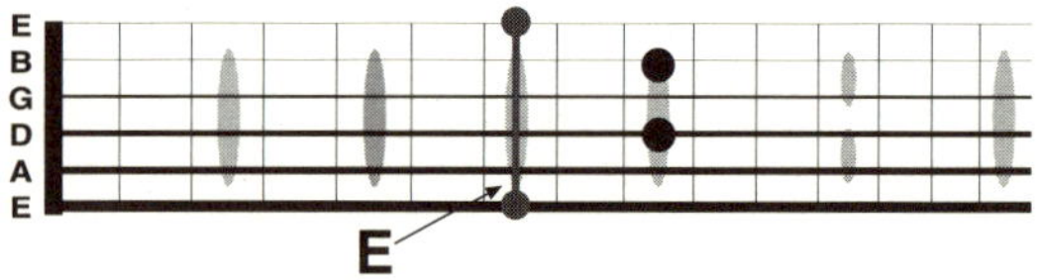

Barred Chords for the Key of A

Again, fingerings are the same as in C. They have just been moved three frets because an A is three half steps lower than a C (A to B♭ to B to C).

Concepts Covered in the Remainder of the Guitar Method

Using barre chords to play rhythm and the rectangle system to solo, you can play 12-bar blues in any key and sound darn good. You will be a musician. The only problem is that after a while you'll lose your self-infatuation and realize you sound pretty much the same all the time because your repertoire of licks, sounds and rhythms is limited. The remainder of the method for guitars involves expanding that repertoire by teaching you ways to produce different sounds and rhythms.

The goal of the Garage Band method for guitar is to bring you to a basic level of competence playing the blues, providing you with skills roughly equivalent to those acquired in a year's time by the saxophonist in the preceding chapters. To reach that level, you need to understand and be able to use the following tools and concepts. The items in the first list you'll recall from the end of the last chapter on the saxophone. They're similar for both instruments.

- The Full Blues Scale
- A Vocabulary of Riffs
- Reading Music
- Major Blues
- Vertical Soloing
- Solo Transcriptions
- Different Chord Progressions
- Solo Shaping

Guitar players also need to focus closely on:

1. **Minor Chords:** As a novice, you start out playing dominant chords with a "major" third tone in them. Later you need to learn the more mysterious sound of chords with a "minor" third, which is a half-step lower than a major third. Minor chords are used in tunes like Santana's *Black Magic Woman* and *Evil Ways.*

2. **Different Rhythms and Time Signatures**: As we've said before, you can to take an old tune and make it sound like a new one by chang-

ing the rhythm. A broad knowledge of this ability is particularly important for members of the rhythm section, who create and maintain the feel of a tune. So, you need to learn how to build your vocabulary of rhythms by stealing them from a variety of sources; how to create your own rhythms; and how some rhythmic differences are described by different time signatures.

3. **Reading Rhythms and Guitar Tablature**: While most instruments rely on standard musical notation, the guitar's nature and its role as a rhythm instrument make it easier for guitarists to read rhythm and tablature notation designed specifically for them. Most guitarists don't read any kind of notation while playing, but you'll be way ahead if you can at least use reading as a tool to help you learn and remember tunes, riffs, scales, etc.

4. **Other Techniques:** Finally, the guitarist's basic bag of tricks should include several techniques used by each hand to add different sounds to both rhythm and solos. For the right hand, this means different ways of picking strings. For the fret hand, it means such things as "hammering on," "pull-offs" and "slides," which are different ways of playing notes on the neck of the guitar with the fingers of the fret hand.

Again, we could try to write out in detail how to do all these things, but putting it on paper is crazy. A lot of this stuff must be *shown* if the average person is going to understand it quickly. By far the quickest way to learn is from a friend or a teacher. We've written this book so you can show it to that friend or teacher and get him or her to show you the things you need to know to play.

How Long Does All This Take?

Gaining a basic command of an electric guitar goes more quickly than the same regime on a sax because of the repetitive way you play a guitar in different keys. Most people should be able to do it and form a

A Note on Nomenclature

Once you go looking for a teacher or guitar-playing friends to show you this stuff, you are likely to find that not everybody calls everything by the same name or does everything the same way. For example, you're likely to find your guitar teacher doesn't use the full six-note blues scale, but a five-note version called the minor pentatonic scale, which is a blues scale with one note left out.

We stick with the blues scale because that's where we started in the chapter on the sax, and we're trying to keep this stuff simple. If your guitar teacher wants to use the minor pentatonic instead, that's fine. Don't argue. You may also find that the term "major blues" raises a few eyebrows. Your guitar teacher may think of what we call major blues as soloing with a major pentatonic scale. Again, that's fine if he or she can explain the concept that way. What's important is that you learn to play major blues, whatever you call it. We just like the term major blues because it sounds simple to us.

blues, rock or country band with players of similar ability in six months to a year. By the end of another year, you and your friends should be able to get a gig in the lounge at your local Holiday Inn (and other, more appealing places). Really. There are lots of working musicians who know less than what we've described. They're not great musicians, but they work and have fun, and people listen to them.

SUMMARY OF THE GARAGE BAND APPROACH TO THE GUITAR

1. Learn how to hold a guitar and how it works.
2. Learn that the guitar has two functions, as a solo instrument and a rhythm instrument.
3. Learn to improvise solos in the key of A along with a recorded rhythm section using the abbreviated, four-note version of the blues scale that we call a rectangle. (See the explanation earlier in the chapter.)
4. Learn to improvise solos in all other keys by moving the starting position of the rectangle to different positions on the fret board (with the ring finger on the root note of the key you want to play).
5. Learn the 12-bar blues form and how it is constructed around what musicians call the I, IV and V chords.
6. Learn easy-to-play, two-string versions of the I, IV and V chords in the key of A.
7. Learn to play the I, IV and V chords in a shuffle rhythm along with a recorded rhythm section of a 12-bar blues.
8. Build a repertoire as a rhythm player by learning to play three additional rhythms:
   — The Jimmy-Reed-style alternative version of the basic shuffle, which Jimmy used it in so many of his songs, including

SUMMARY, continued...

Bright Lights, Big City and *Baby What You Want Me to Do*;

— The Chuck-Berry-style rock rhythm, which Chuck used in songs like *Oh Baby Doll*; and

— An alternative version of the rock rhythm, which Jimmy Reed used in songs like *Shame Shame Shame* and *I'm Going to Upside Your Head*. (The basic rhythms are illustrated in guitar tablature in the appendices.)

9. Learn to play the I, IV and V chords in all other keys by moving the finger patterns for the chords in the key of A to other positions on the fret board.
10. Learn to play the I, IV and V chords in D as barre chords.
11. Learn to translate the D barre chords to all other keys.
12. Learn to solo using the full blues scale.
13. Learn to get a different solo sound by playing what we call major blues, i.e., by soloing on the blues scale from the related minor key rather than the key in which you are playing.
14. Learn to play tunes with different chord progressions than the basic 12-bar blues.
15. Learn how to develop a vocabulary of riffs for soloing.
16. Learn a different solo sound called vertical soloing, in which you focus on the chord tones rather than scale tones.
17. Learn to shape solos using dynamics, velocity, etc., so the solos have a beginning, middle and end.
18. Learn the basics of reading musical notation as well as guitar tablature (well enough to make notes for yourself and learn tunes by reading them).
19. Learn how to read transcriptions of great solos to learn the licks of great players.

SUMMARY, continued . . .

20. Learn to get a different rhythm and/or solo sound by playing minor chords.
21. Learn how to develop a repertoire of the different rhythms for the kind of tunes you like to play.
22. Learn about time signatures and how they are used to describe certain rhythmic characteristics of a tune.
23. Learn several techniques for picking with the right hand and for playing notes on the neck with the fret hand (slides, hammering on, and pull-offs).

10

THE PIANO Part 1

When most people think of piano playing, they think of a lone pianist like Billy Joel or Elton John, whose two hands must do all the work, the left hand playing bass line on the low notes and the right hand playing melody on the high notes. That's a scary thought for most people, because our lives usually don't require us to do different tasks with our two hands.

One of the many nice things about the piano is that you don't *have to* play alone. For novices, it's a lot more fun to play in a band or along with a recorded rhythm section. When you do that, you can divide the tasks of each hand and conquer them one at a time.

Our Piano Man

Blues pianist Ken Harris helped write this section. Ken is co-owner of one of the West's finest blues venues, Boise's Blues Bouquet, which features musicians ranging from local talent to such household names as Charlie Musselwhite and Jimmy Rogers. Before settling down in the house band at the Bouquet, Ken made his living for more than 20 years playing in blues and R&B bands in Boston. He's played with Junior Walker, Chuck Berry and Luther "Guitar Jr." Johnson.

Ken Harris

Tackle the Rhythm and Solo Tracks One at a Time

In a band, the piano player is a lot like the rhythm guitarist. He or she spends three-fourths of his or her career playing rhythm, helping the bassist and drummer hold down the bottom of the groove. The pianist takes his or her turn soloing just like everyone else, letting the other members of the rhythm section carry the bottom while he or she creates a melody. Once you break the chore of piano playing down into these basic components – rhythm and solo – the Garage Band approach for piano is much like that for guitar.

The Rhythm Track – Comping

Like the guitarist, a piano player needs to know the basics of the 12-bar blues form. As a piano player, you want to quickly get into the responsible role of what pianists call "comping," playing rhythm with both hands as part of the rhythm section. To start you into that role, the teacher has to make sure you know the little bit of music theory needed to understand 12-bar blues (which we've already discussed):

- A little about chords in general;
- A little about the I, IV and V chords in particular; and
- How the three chords fall into the 12-bar form.

Playing Piano Chords an Easy Way

To get you started playing these chords, the Garage Band method does the same thing for piano that it did for guitar, reducing the I, IV and V chords to a simple, easy-to-play form in a single key. The chords usually played by blues bands have four notes in them, but you don't have to start out playing all four of the notes. Like the guitarist, you can start with two notes, which is easy and still sounds great. We start with the key of C, which is the easiest key on the piano because the white keys are the notes of the C major scale.

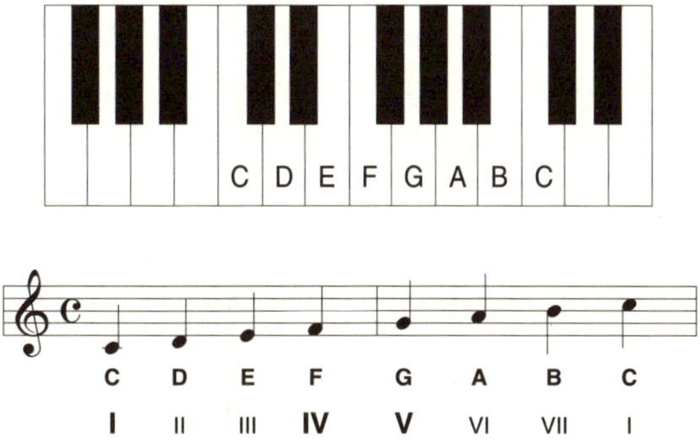

C Major Scale

The I, IV and V chords for the left hand are shown in the next diagram. The pinkie plays the root while the thumb plays the fifth of the chord. (The fifth is just the fifth note of the major scale that begins with the root.)

C Chord for the Left Hand

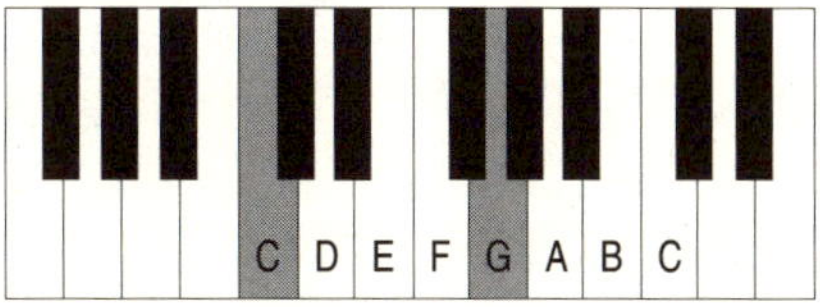

F Chord for the Left Hand

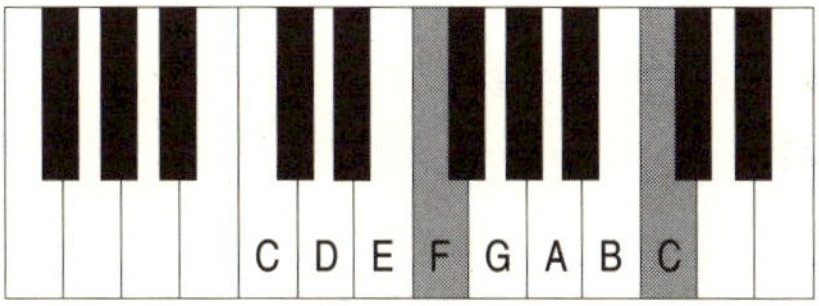

G Chord for the Left Hand

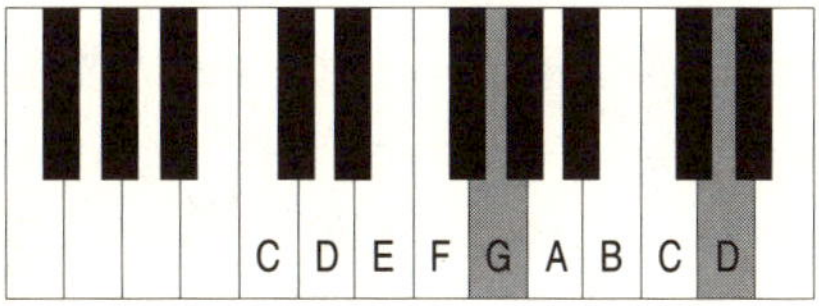

You'll recall from the discussion of rhythm guitar that the new guitarist quickly learns how to play the simple I, IV and V chords in two versions of a blues shuffle rhythm and two versions of the Chuck Berry rock 'n' roll rhythm. With that modest repertoire of rhythms, the guitarist can play rhythm on hundreds of tunes.

You'll do the same thing on piano, but at a slightly slower pace. As soon as you learn the easy chords shown in the diagram, which will take just a few minutes, you'll learn how to play them in one of the same shuffle rhythm patterns learned by the guitarist (shown in the key of C in Appendix 6). You'll go home, practice that pattern along with your 12-bar-blues recording and come back to the next lesson able to play the rhythm pattern pretty smoothly with your left hand.

What You Just Learned in the Key of C

Your Left Hand	Your Right Hand
Plays a simple chord in the basic shuffle pattern.	Relaxes

Comping

At this point, you'll know how to play half of each chord with your left hand. The next step is to learn to play the other half of the C, F and G chords with the right hand in an even simpler way so the right hand can play rhythm along with the left to give you a fuller sound. If you have to think about what you're doing with your left hand, you want a no-brain task for your right. Fortunately, there is a *very* simple way to play the other half of the chords with the right hand, as show in the following diagram.

No-brain C Chord for the Right Hand

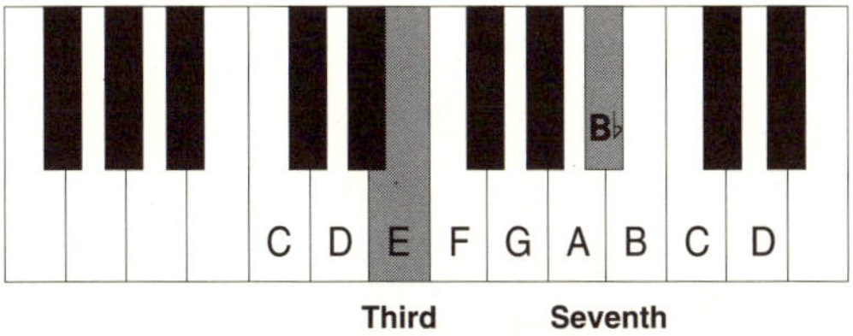

No-brain F Chord for the Right Hand

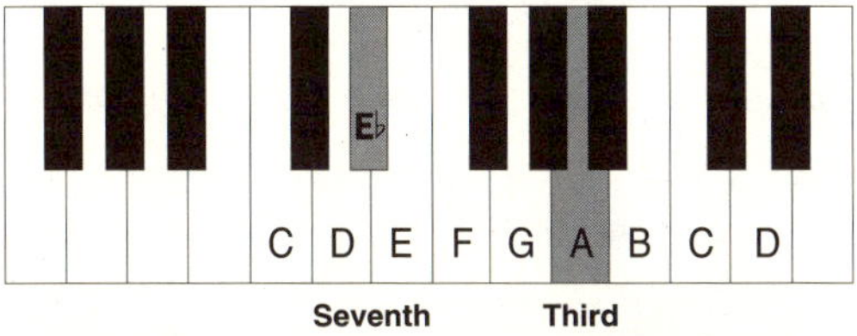

No-brain G Chord for the Right Hand

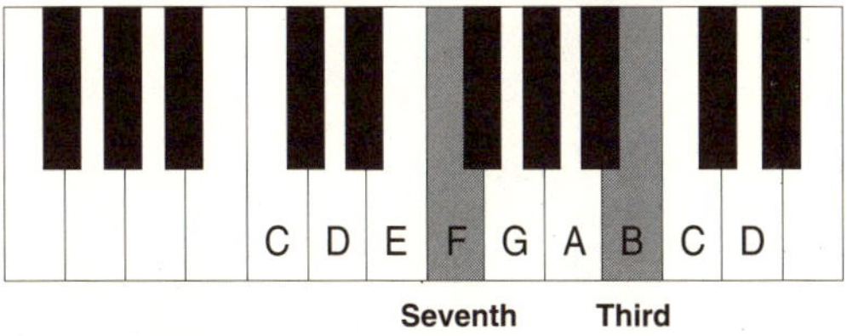

The beauty of these chords is that if you start out playing the no-brain C chord, then all you have to do to get to the no-brain F chord is move your fingers down the keyboard (left) one key. To move from the no-brain C chord to the no-brain G chord, all you have to do is move your fingers up the keyboard (right) one key. They're all right next to each other.

Once you learn to play these forms of the chords, which will take just a few minutes at the piano, you can combine them with what you've already learned for the left hand. You'll do that by playing the basic rhythm pattern with the left hand and simply striking the right hand half of the chord on the first beat of the rhythm pattern. If you go home and practice this for 20 minutes a night, moving from chord to chord along with the recorded rhythm section, you'll be able to do it pretty well in a week. When you get to that point you'll sound like a blues train coming down the track. (No kidding.)

What You Just Learned in the Key of C

<u>Your Left Hand</u>	<u>Your Right Hand</u>
Plays a simple chord in the basic shuffle rhythm pattern.	Plays the no-brain chord on the first beat of the pattern.

A Little Music Theory

You have just learned how to use both your hands to play some chords on the piano. You will move from here more quickly if you understand a little of the theory behind what you've learned. As we said, the four-note chords we've described are the kind often played by blues bands. They're called "dominant seventh chords". They're constructed from the major scale that begins with the root note of the chord. The components of the chord are the root, the third, the fifth and the flatted (lowered) seventh of the major scale.

C Major Scale

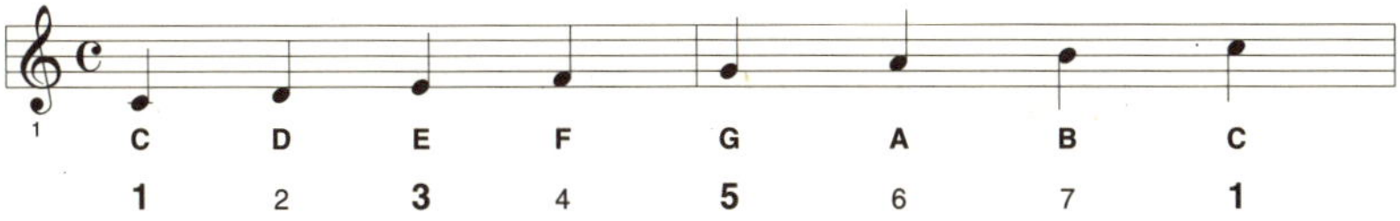

As you can see from the diagram, the root of the C major scale is C, the third is E and the fifth is G. The seventh is B, so the flatted or lowered seventh is B♭. (For ease of understanding, we call this lowered seventh the dominant seventh even though some niggling theorists may point out that that's not quite right.) The four notes of the C dominant seventh chord are C, E, G and B♭.

These notes are shown in the following diagram of the piano keyboard.

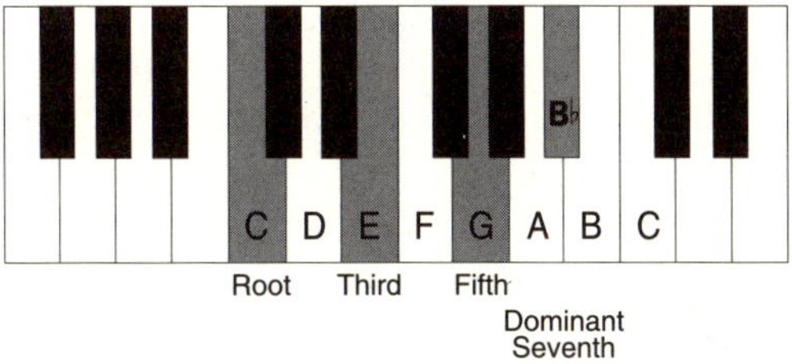

The Tones in a C Dominant Seventh Chord

An accomplished pianist often will play all the chord tones with one hand. This is a little bit hard for a novice, especially when you start trying to move from chord to chord. It is a lot easier to play two of the chord tones with each hand, as we've already discussed, which still sounds good and makes it a lot simpler to move from chord to chord. What you're doing in that case is playing the root and fifth with the left hand and the third and seventh with the right, as shown in the following diagram, which is a cool thing to do.

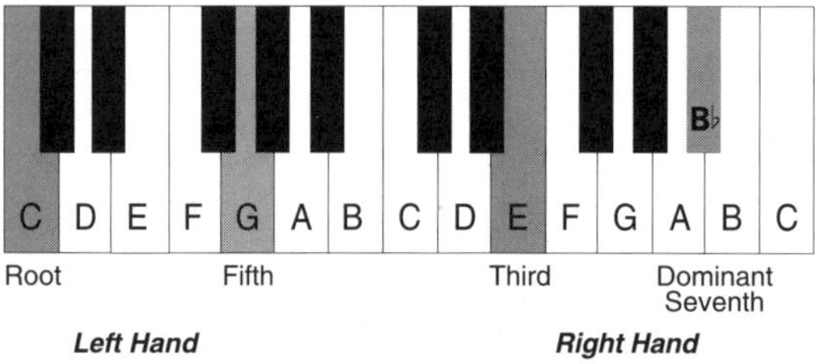

The C Dominant Seventh Chord Played with Two Hands

You're doing the same thing when you play the F dominant seventh chord and the G dominant seventh chord the way we showed you.

F Major Scale

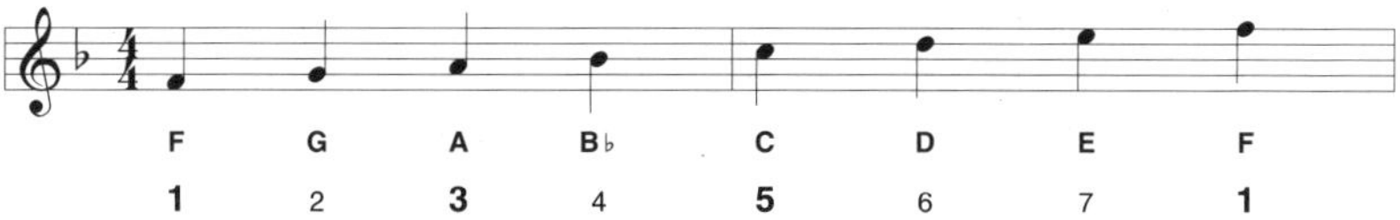

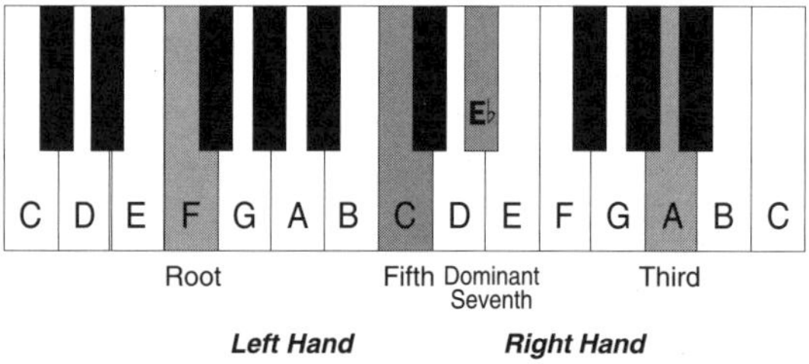

The F Dominant Seventh Chord Played withTwo Hands

G Major Scale

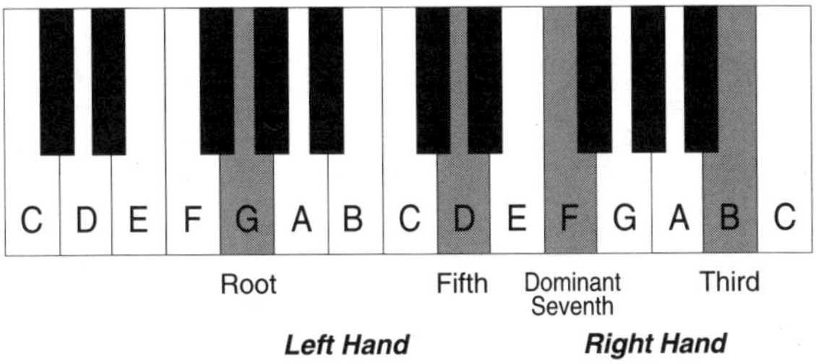

The G Dominant Seventh Chord Played withTwo Hands

You can construct and play the I, IV and V dominant seventh chords in any key the same way.

Other Kinds of Keyboard Instruments

Before we go any further, we should say a word about the qualities of various kinds of keyboard instruments. They are not created equal. In fact, they come in three basic classes.

Weighted-Action Keyboards: This includes regular acoustic pianos and electronic keyboards that are designed to feel like pianos to the touch. Play a note on a piano, and you can feel the weight you have to push. It's there because a piano key moves a lever that moves a hammer that strikes a string to make a tone. The volume of the tone depends on how hard you strike the key. Almost as important, a pianist has to work with the "bounce" of the hammer to re-strike a tone, which imposes a natural rhythmic feel on the piano keyboard. Electronic keyboards with a weighted action are designed to match these qualities.

Touch-Sensitive Keyboards: These electronic keyboards don't resist when you push a key, but the volume does depend on how hard you strike the key.

Non-Touch-Sensitive Keyboards: The keys of these instruments are basically on-off switches. You push down the key, and the note starts at the volume you've selected with the volume knob. You let off the key, the note stops.

Our first preference for beginners is an acoustic piano for two reasons. First, its weighted action allows you an infinite variety of tonal qualities based on how you strike and mix notes. Second, the "feel" of the weighted action lends itself to playing the blues stylistically and rhythmically because that's where the feel of piano blues came from – being played on the keyboard of a real piano.

Our second choice, for those who want something more portable, is a touch-sensitive electronic keyboard with a weighted action. Our preference here is based on the same reasons as our bias toward acoustic pianos.

If you can't get a piano or weighted-action keyboard, you should at the very least get a keyboard that is touch-sensitive. If you can't control the volume of individual notes, you are giving up a huge part of the keyboard's ability to make music subtle and interesting. Non-touch-sensitive keyboards are way better than nothing, but are only for those folks who don't have any other choice.

11

THE PIANO: Part 2

At this point, you are two or three weeks into the Garage Band method for piano and, if you've been practicing 20 minutes or so a day, you will be able to play C blues with another musician by comping with both hands, laying down a rhythm for your friend or friends to solo over. I know you can, because I tried it. A month ago[1] I couldn't play the piano at all. Then, our piano man, Ken Harris, taught me what's been described so far. I practiced a little every day and, last week, played the basic shuffle rhythm on the piano for one of my guitarist friends while he improvised solos. It's crazy how simple this stuff is if you approach it the right way – particularly if you have someone to play along with.

Unfortunately, you won't be satisfied for long just playing one shuffle rhythm in the key of C. Music is one of those pursuits where you can't stand still. Most people have to keep

Listen to Music Every day

As we've said before, you should always always always be listening to the music of the players you want to sound like. Some good mentors for blues piano are Otis Spann, Memphis Slim, Honey Piazza and Pinetop Perkins.

[1]February 1995

progressing or they get bored. The next step in the process for the piano is starting to solo.

At First, You'll Play Rhythm More Than Solo

On the piano, playing rhythm with two hands is a lot easier than playing a solo or melody with your right hand while trying to keep a rhythm going with your left. It's more than possible to start playing rhythm piano with a blues band in a few weeks. You can sound darn good in a few months. That's why you'll want to focus on playing rhythm at first, because it's so much fun to succeed so quickly. The secret to having the same success with solos at the outset is to keep them simple, letting the left hand rest while your right hand plays two- or three-note licks with energy and feeling. Listen hard to the recordings of players like Memphis Slim, Honey Piazza and Otis Spann to hear how simple, repetitive licks can make a tune rock.

The Solo Track

When you start to solo, you're going to want to keep things simple at first. The way to do that is to go back to using just one hand – the right, this time. You'll do the same thing as the saxophonist – learning one octave of the C blues scale, which is shown in the diagram below.

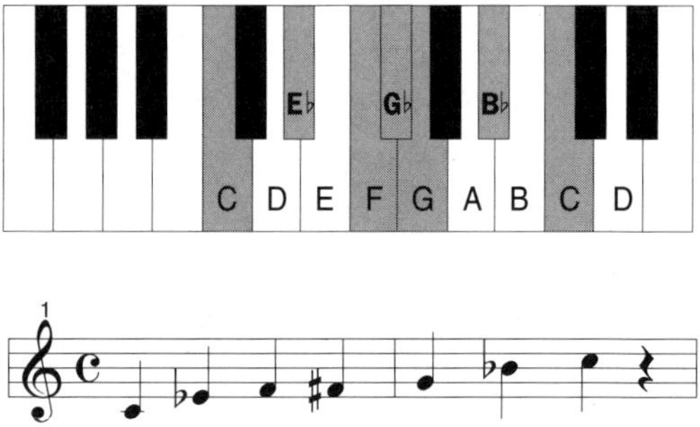

C Blues Scale

Like the saxophonist, you'll learn how to groove along with the recorded rhythm section by turning a few notes from the blues scale into simple riffs. Just as with the sax and guitar, the key is to start simple and play in rhythm. You can start with any three or four notes of the scale at the beginning, playing them in any rhythmic way you like until you start to develop simple riffs, which will happen because the sounds of the blues scale are so intuitive. When you start to feel comfortable with those three or four notes, you can expand to the full scale.

What You Just Learned in the Key of C

Your Left Hand	Your Right Hand
Relaxes	Solos along with a recording, using a few notes of the blues scale.

Using Both Hands Again

Once you go home and practice your right-hand soloing for a week, you'll be ready to add the left hand back into the action. What you'll want your left hand to do is play rhythm using the root-fifth form of each chord while your right hand solos. You could do this by playing the root-fifth forms of the chords that we've already shown you – the ones shown again in the following diagram.

C Chord for the Left Hand

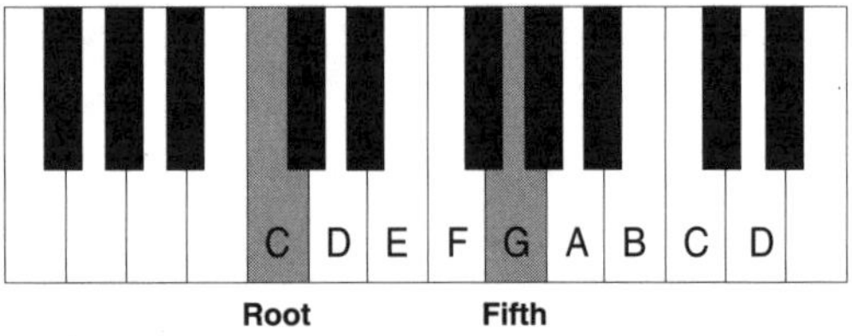

F Chord for the Left Hand

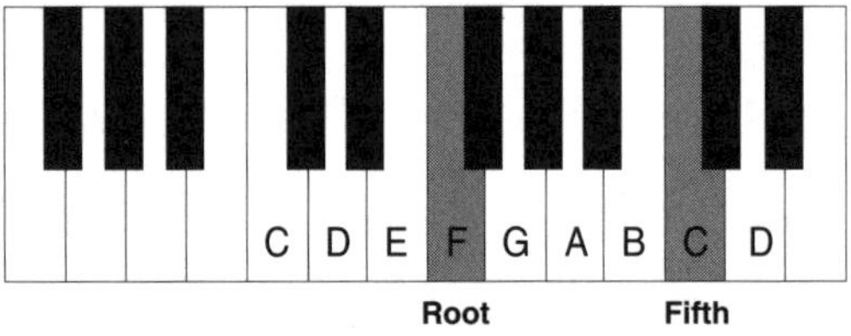

G Chord for the Left Hand

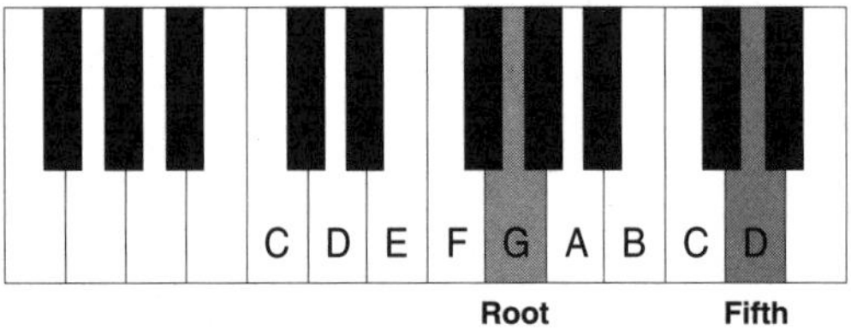

However, that requires a little bit too much mental activity for a novice who's trying to improvise with his or her right hand – because it is such a long jump down the keyboard from the C chord to the F chord or G chord. What would be nice to know is a way to play all three of these chords without moving your fingers very far, the way you did with the right-hand chords in the discussion on comping.

Fortunately, there's a way to do just that. If you look at the notes of the F and G chords in the diagram above, you'll see they are right next to each other. Now, look in the next diagram at what happens if you "invert" the C chord and think of it as a fifth and a root instead of a root and a fifth.

No-brain C Chord for the Left Hand

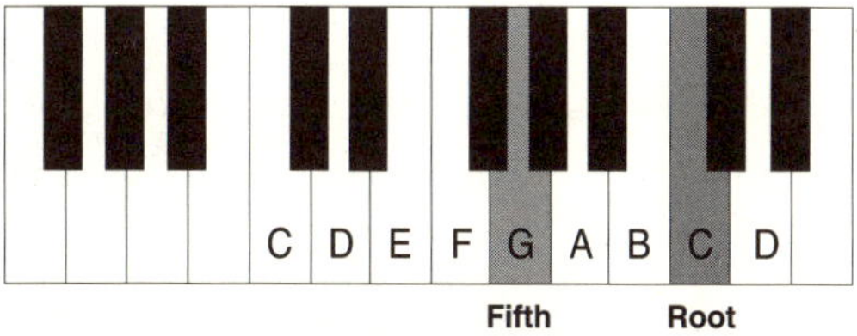

No-brain F Chord for the Left Hand

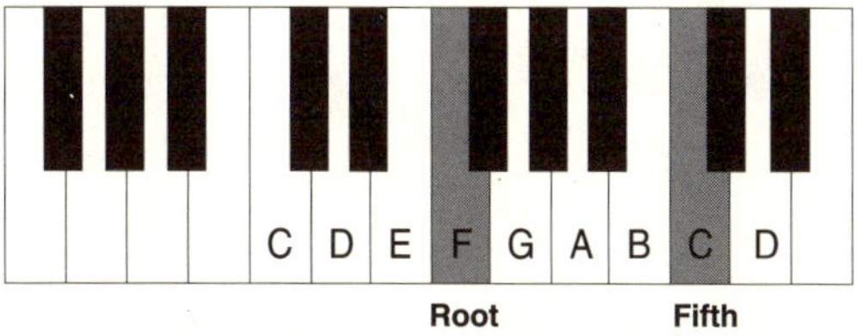

No-brain G Chord for the Left Hand

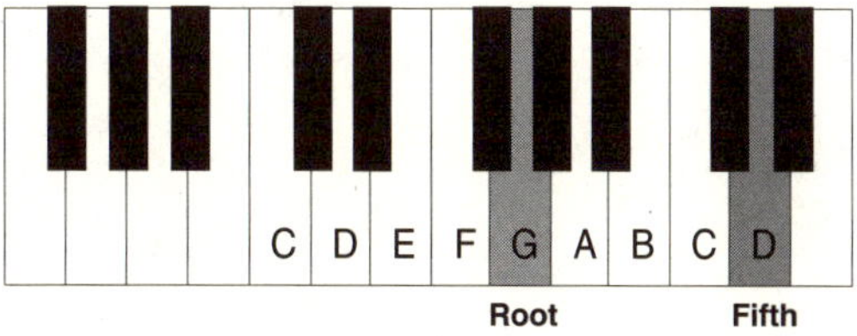

Now all three chords are right next to each other. If you start out playing the C chord this way, with your pinkie on the fifth and your thumb on the root, all you have to do is move your pinkie one white key to the left to be playing the F chord. To move from the C chord to the G chord, all you have to do is move your thumb from the C to the D. Pretty easy.

However, even that requires too much mental activity if you try to play our basic shuffle rhythm with the left hand while still learning to solo with the right. Since you now have to think about your right hand, you need a no-brain activity for your left hand. So what you'll want to do is simply play the left-hand root-fifth form of the appropriate chord at the beginning of each bar, then hold it down while improvising over the blues scale with your right hand.

You can play these versions of the left-hand chords while soloing with the right hand over the C blues scale, because using these forms of the chords really is a no-brainer. At first, you will, of course, want to do this along with the recorded rhythm section, because that makes it more fun.

What You Just Learned in the Key of C

Your Left Hand	Your Right Hand
Plays a no-brain chord at the start of each measure.	Solos using a few notes of the blues scale.

Inversions

What you've just learned about "inverting" a chord makes moving from chord to chord way easier. As you may already have guessed, we used the inversion trick without telling you in the last chapter when we explained the right hand chords used to comp. If you look at the next diagram, which shows the right-hand chords you learned in the last chapter for playing rhythm, you'll see the C chord is a third-seventh inversion while the F and G chords are seventh-third inversions.

No-brain C Chord for the Right Hand

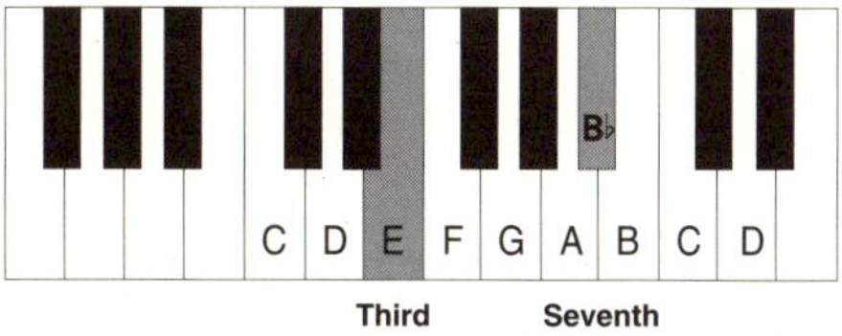

No-brain F Chord for the Right Hand

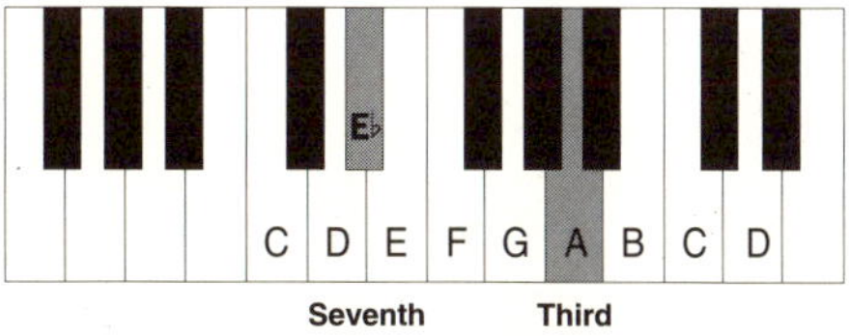

No-brain G Chord for the Right Hand

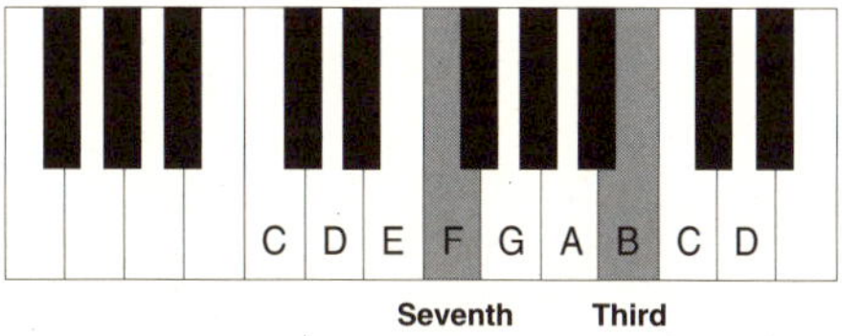

You can use this trick with the I, IV and V chords in any key.

Here's what you learned in the key of C

- The I, IV and V chords.
- How to comp along with a recorded rhythm section using the basic shuffle rhythm pattern with the left hand while striking the no-brain third-seventh inversion of the chord with the right hand.
- How to solo along with a recorded rhythm section using the blues scale with the right hand and no-brain root-fifth inversions of the chord with the left hand.

12

THE PIANO Part 3

Everything we've described thus far for the piano should take more or less a month to cover. The process then starts repeating itself. You'll do basically the same thing in each key.

You will discover that the second key – G – goes faster than the first one. That's because playing the left-hand rhythm in G is just like playing it in C. You just move the pattern a little way down the keyboard. Again, the I, IV and V chords are based on the first, fourth and fifth notes of the G major scale, which are G, C and D. The root-fifth chords are as shown in the next diagram.

G Major Scale

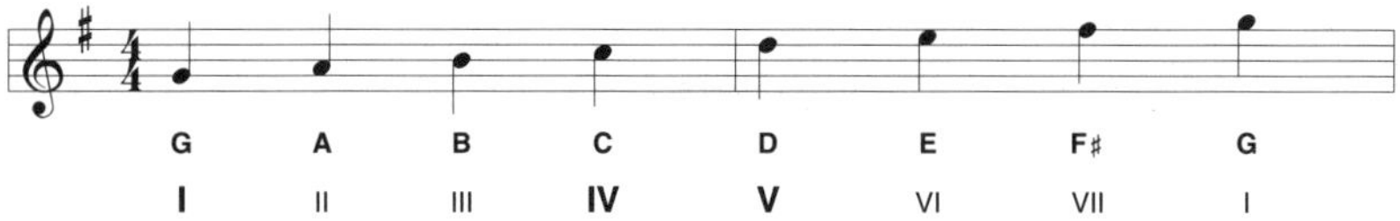

G Chord for the Left Hand (I Chord in G)

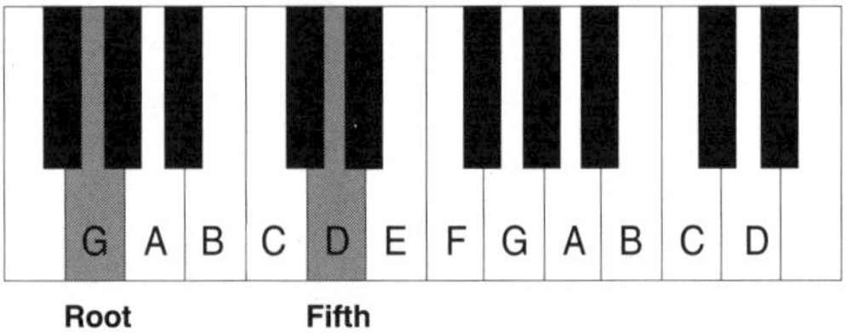

C Chord for the Left Hand (IV Chord in G)

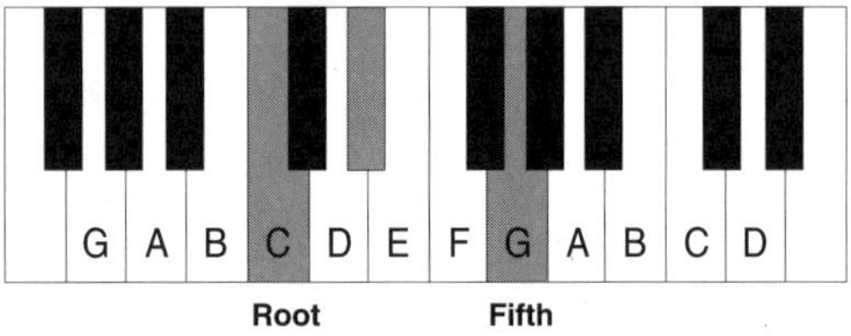

D Chord for the Left Hand (V Chord in G)

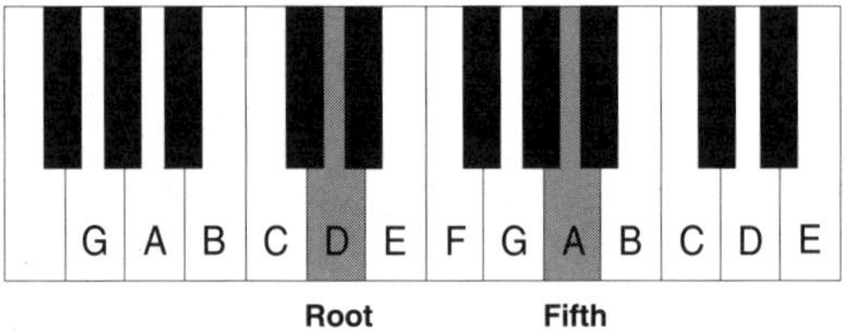

This pattern for the chords with the left hand is the same in all keys. It gets slightly more difficult when you move into keys in which you have to start playing black keys, but even that really doesn't cause much trouble because you don't get to the black keys until you're becoming accustomed to the keyboard.

You will also notice that two of the chords in the key of G – the G chord and C chord – were also used in the key of C.

	Chords for Key of C	Chords for Key of G
I Chord	C	G
IV Chord	F	C
V Chord	G	D

So, you really have to learn only one new chord – the D – to play in the key of G. The same thing happens as you move into each new key – you have to learn only one additional chord.

Doing More With Each Key

Since your left hand doesn't really have much to learn in the key of G, you can add something new to the basics here. Once you realize how easy it is to play the shuffle rhythm pattern in the new key, your teacher will teach you the basic Chuck-Berry-style rock rhythm learned by the novice guitarist in Chapter 8. This additional rhythm will allow you to play dozens more songs. You'll also learn how to use the right hand along with the left at the same lesson. The right will play the no-brain third-seventh inversions of the I, IV and V chords. This, too, will be easy, because these chords are similar to the right-hand chords played in the previous key.

No-brain G Chord for the Right Hand

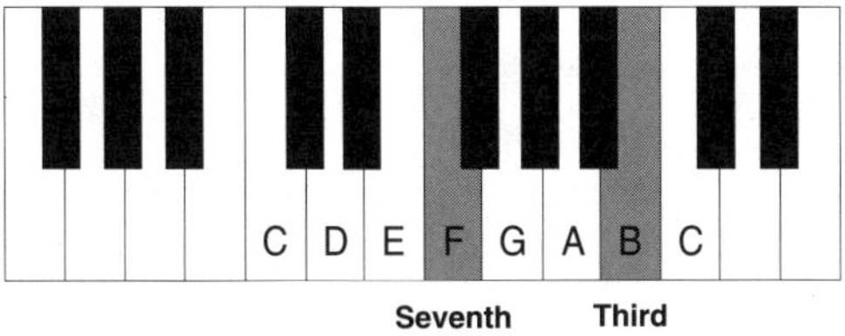

No-brain C Chord for the Right Hand

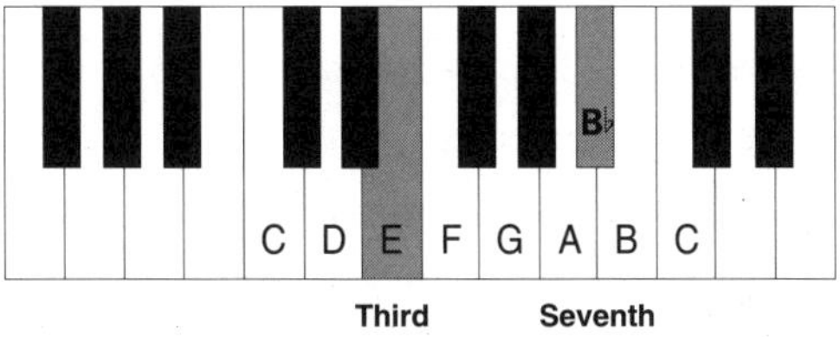

No-brain D Chord for the Right Hand

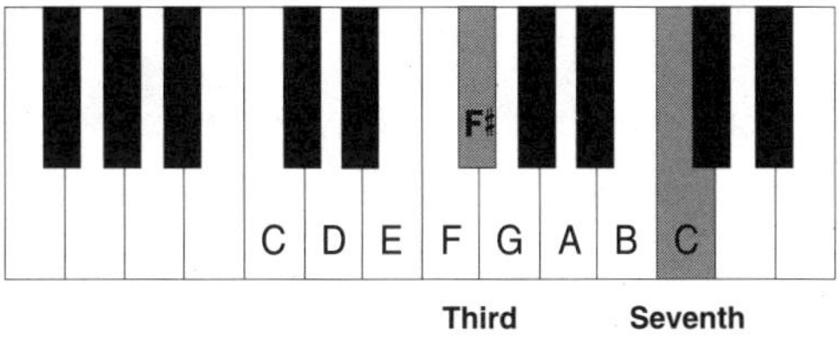

After you go home and practice for another week, you'll be able to comp in both the key of C and the key of G using two rhythms: the basic shuffle and the basic rock rhythm. You'll be able to play blues in these keys with other musicians, and will be starting to get a feel for the 12-bar-blues form, which makes it a good time to start learning to play simple blues melodies with your right hand.

What You Just Learned in the Key of G

Your Left Hand	Your Right Hand
Plays a simple chord in the basic rock rhythm. or Plays a simple chord in the basic shuffle rhythm pattern.	Plays a no-brain third-seventh chord on the first beat of each measure.

Learning to Play Melodies

We start Garage Band pianists with a standard slow blues like *Stormy Monday*. When you're ready, your teacher will show you how to play the melody by ear and memory, using just your right hand. (He or she also will give you the written melody, just to help you remember it. You should be able to play the tune by ear and memory within a short time.)

Once you can grope your way through the melody with right hand, the teacher will show you how to add the left hand. You won't use the basic shuffle rhythm, however. That's too hard for a novice trying to play a melody with the right hand. Instead, the teacher will show you how to play the no-brain root-fifth inversions of the I, IV and V chords with the left hand at the beginning of each bar, the same way you did in the key of C when improvising over the C blues scale with your right hand.

No-brain G Chord for the Left Hand

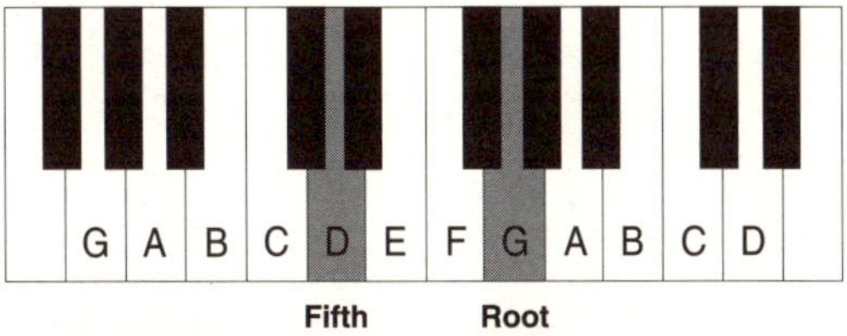

No-brain C Chord for the Left Hand

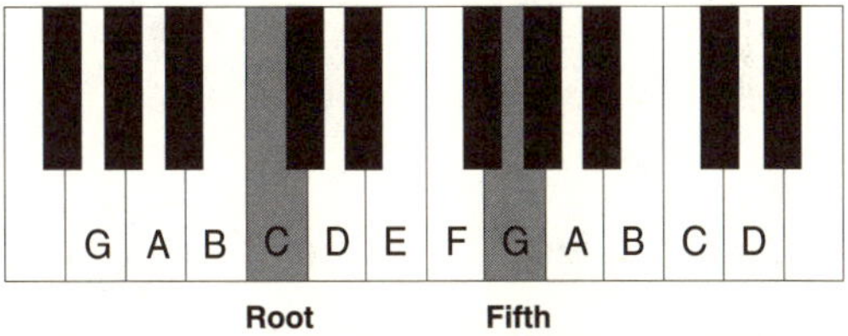

No-brain D Chord for the Left Hand

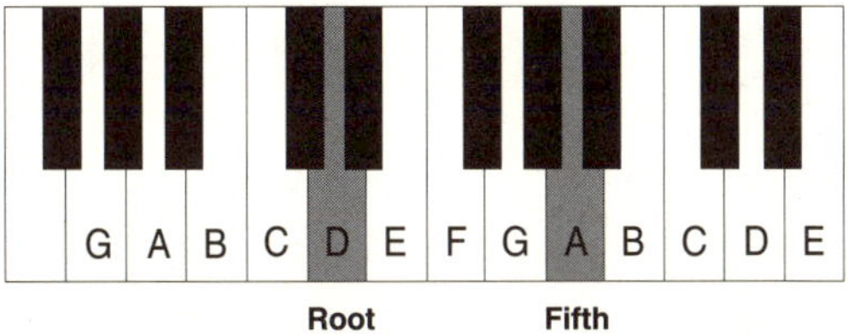

The Remainder of the Key of G

To finish off the key of G, you will learn how to improvise solos using the G blues scale. As in the key of C, you'll first learn the blues scale with the right hand alone, then add the left hand playing the no-brain inversions of the root-fifth chords. Once you go home and practice that for a week, you will have basic blues in the key of G pretty much under control.

What You Just Learned in the Key of G

Your Left Hand	Your Right Hand
Plays a no-brain root-fifth chord at the beginning of each measure.	Plays a simple blues melody like *Stormy Monday.* *or* Solos using the G blues scale.

Then You Just Do the Same Things in the Other Keys

In the remainder of the Garage Band method for the piano, you'll get down the basics one key at a time by learning the same things you learned in the key of G:

- The major scale and I, IV and V chords.
- How to comp with both hands in a shuffle rhythm and a rock rhythm.
- The blues scale and how to improvise solos with it.
- A blues melody (played with the right hand while playing the no-brain chords with the left hand).

With that knowledge, you'll do the following in each key.

When Your Left Hand Plays	Your Right Hand Will Play
Basic shuffle pattern	No-brain third-seventh inversions
Basic rock pattern	No-brain third-seventh inversions
No-brain root-fifth inversions	Solo on blues scale
No-brain root-fifth inversions	Melody

Learning these basics for each key provides the foundation for playing blues piano. As you master these skills in each key, you'll pick up the other concepts and techniques you need to play blues with your friends. You'll find that each key goes a little more quickly than the one before it, because the rhythm patterns are similar in every key.

Other Concepts

In addition to the basics of each key, the teacher also will cover some additional concepts one at a time throughout the year to provide you the rest of the tools needed to play in your average local blues band. The items on the list below are the same for the piano as for the sax and guitar.

A vocabulary of riffs	Major blues	Different chord progressions
Reading music	Vertical soloing	Solo shaping
Minor chords		

Pianists also will need to spend time on some additional tools:

1. Different Rhythm Patterns: Once you get comfortable with the basic shuffle and rock rhythms, your teacher will show you other rhythms for both your left and right hands. He or she will first add variations of the two original rhythms for your left hand, then will go on to several left-hand rhythms with a different feel. For the right hand, you will learn to sometimes play the same rhythm as the left hand. Your teacher should also show you some different right-hand rhythms that complement what's going on with the left hand.

2. Other Inversions: Thus far, you've been playing root-fifth chords with the left hand when soloing or playing a melody with the right. Your teacher will show you how you can get a different sound by playing third-seventh inversions with the left hand (These are the same chords you've been using in the right hand, just lower down the keyboard). Eventually, the teacher will show you how you rearrange the components of any chord into any number of combinations to get different sounds or to make a tune easier to play.

3. Additional Chord Tones: Once you've gone through three or four keys and start getting more comfortable with the keyboard, the teacher can show you how to add a root or fifth to the third-seventh inversions you've been playing when comping with the right hand. The teacher eventually will want to do the same thing with the left hand, adding a third or a seventh to the two-note root-fifth chords played by the left hand. One thing to remember about chords, however, is that more notes is not necessarily better. Sometimes the two-note chords you've already learned will be the best possible choice because they sound the best for a certain situation. In other situations, adding more chord tones may be desirable. What's important is what sounds best.

4. Grace notes: When it comes to one element of the blues, pianos are at a disadvantage compared with instruments like a sax or guitar. On a sax or guitar, you can *bend* notes to change their pitch and get a bluesy sound. Obviously, you can't do that on a piano. What your teacher can show you as a substitute is how to use something called a *grace note* to get a similar effect. A grace note is simply a note that is a half-step up or down from one of the notes in the riff you're playing. You get the bending effect by starting on the grace note and sliding quickly to the actual note in your riff.

SUMMARY OF THE GARAGE BAND APPROACH TO THE PIANO

1. Learn how to sit at the piano and how it works.
2. Learn a little basic music notation.
3. Learn the notes on the keyboard.

The key of C

4. Learn the C major scale.
5. Learn the chord structure of a basic 12-bar blues.
6. Learn how to play the root-five form of the I, IV and V chords in the key of C with the left hand in our basic shuffle rhythm.
7. Learn how to comp along with a 12-bar blues recording with the left hand, using what you just learned.
8. Learn how to use inversions to play the third-seventh form of the I, IV and V chords in the key of C with the right hand in a no-brain version of the shuffle rhythm, i.e., by playing the chord on the first beat of each measure of the tune.
9. Learn how to play the left-hand rhythm and the right-hand rhythm simultaneously.
10. Learn the names and relationships of the notes of the I, IV and V chords.
11. Learn to play one octave of the C blues scale with the right hand.
12. Learn how to solo along with a recorded rhythm section with the right hand, using the C blues scale.
13. Learn how to use inversions to play the root-five and third-seventh forms of the I, IV and V chords in the key of C with the left hand in a no-brain version of the shuffle rhythm.
14. Learn how to solo with the right hand, using the C blues scale, while comping with the left hand, using a no-brain

version of the shuffle rhythm.

The key of G.

15. Repeat all of the above steps for the key of G.
16. Learn to do all the same things using a Chuck-Berry-style rock rhythm instead of the basic shuffle.
17. Learn to play the melody of a 12-bar blues tune in G, first with the right hand alone, then with the left hand comping the no-brain rhythm.

The key of D

18. Repeat all of the above steps for the key of D minor, learning the minor I, IV and V chords and how they are formed.

The key of A

19. Repeat all of the above steps for the key of A.
20. Learn how to add a root or fifth to the third-seventh inversion of the chords played by the right hand.
21. Learn how to use the A blues scale to solo in the key of C to get a "major blues" sound.

The key of E

22. Repeat all of the above steps for the key of E.
23. Learn variations of the basic left-hand shuffle and rock rhythms that add a dominant seventh to them.

The remaining keys

24. Repeat all of the above steps for each of the remaining keys. As you learn each key, study one or more of the following:
    — How to develop a vocabulary of riffs.
    — How to develop a vocabulary of rhythm patterns for comping and soloing.
    — More about reading music.
    — How to solo vertically over chord tones.
    — How to shape solos.
    — How to play different chord progressions.
    — How to expand the use of chord inversions.
    — How and when to add additional chord tones to the chords played by the right and left hand.
    — How to use grace notes.

13

WHERE DO I GO FROM HERE?

Once you complete the Garage Band basics, you will possess a lot of musical knowledge and skills. You'll know your instrument. You'll know your major and blues scales in all 12 keys. You'll know your major chords in all 12 keys. You'll know how to improvise blues solos in all 12 keys. You'll understand the basic blues form well enough so that you can easily teach yourself variations of it (meaning you can easily learn to play and improvise any songs in the Western world's vast repertoire of simple music, i.e. rock, reggae, blues, folk, country and their close relatives.) You will know how to play with other musicians. You'll know at least a half-dozen common blues tunes and several ballads (all taught by your teacher). You'll know a number of other tunes that you've learned yourself or with friends. You'll have a small repertoire of riffs. You'll read music (though not well unless you've studied reading elsewhere.)

Perhaps most important, you will know how to learn music. If you and your teacher have done your jobs well, you will be a musical perpetual motion machine. You won't know everything, not even close, but you will know how to find the resources (teachers, friends, books, recordings, videos, etc.) that will put you on course toward any musical goal you want.

If you are like most people, however, you will not be satisfied with this significant accomplishment. You will listen to your playing and say, "Man, I have a long way to go." (This thought, it turns out, has more to do with human nature than with your level of achievement. Even terrific musicians think it.)

Where will you go? That's the question. The answer depends a lot on what kind of music you want to play. If you want to improvise on more complicated tunes – jazz – you will have to learn more jazz theory and scales. If you want to play classical music or read charts with a big band, you'll have to learn to read a lot better. If you want to play Latin music, you'll have to learn new rhythms. If you only want to play blues or rock or country, you'll want to learn more riffs and tunes.

No matter what music you pursue, the additional skills and knowledge you'll want will fall into three broad categories of potential development: 1) Technique; 2) Music Theory; and 3) Style.

Technique

The most obvious need for improvement will be in your technique – your control of the instrument. When you finish the Garage Band basics, you'll be like a 40-pound kid with a 50-pound German shepherd on a leash. You'll do fine so long as the shepherd walks peacefully along the street, but if he goes after a cat, so will your control.

Fortunately, you will be in a good position to improve your technique unassisted. If you're like a lot of people, you may simply decide you won't need any more music lessons at this point. That's a reasonable approach. Just take what you know and use it to play music with your friends, getting better as you learn new songs, having fun and figuring things out for yourself.

The Learning-New-Songs Approach

There's not much to explain about this approach, except that learning songs is more fun if you do it with friends.

The way you go it alone is to teach yourself the melody and chord progression of a tune by listening to a record or reading the tune out of a book. One bit of advice. Don't be discouraged if you at first have a hard time hearing the notes of a melody or riff well enough to repeat them on your instrument. The tendency among relatively inexperienced players is to blame their imagined lack of musical talent for the difficulty of this task. The truth is that hearing and transcribing riffs and solos is slow going for most musicians, even those with lots of experience. You have to be tenacious. That's why the best way to learn songs is from and with friends. You'll often hear one guitar player say something like, "I just can't figure out what Clapton's doing in that part of the song." To which his friend will reply, "I know what you mean. I worked and worked on that and finally found it in *Guitar* magazine. Here. Let me show you."

Playing new songs with friends is probably the most pleasurable way to really learn them and to improve your performance, too. For one thing, your friends will give you attaboys or girls when you do well. They'll also hear things about your playing that you don't – because you're engrossed in playing. They'll often give you tips about how to improve a riff or play it in a better place. They'll also tell you when you screw up, which can be either good or bad depending on how tactful your friends are. (Read the chapter on forming a band to find out more about how you can maximize the constructive part of this musical relationship and minimize the sarcasm and backbiting.)

The bottom line on the learning new songs approach is that the more time you spend on your instrument, the better you will get – up to a point. The upside is that this method is fun all the time. The downside is two-fold. Improvement is relatively slow. And, after a while, most people smack into a ceiling. They know a lot of songs, but they have a limited range of "sounds" (as in, man, I like his sound). Is that bad? Not necessarily. Maybe what you want out of music is to play and sing Hank William Sr. songs like Hank Sr. did. That's a laudable goal, and you can achieve it with this approach.

But what if you want to play Eric Clapton songs the way Eric does? You probably won't get there through this approach, because you can't play like Clapton simply by copying Clapton. You can play the same notes he plays and approximate the feel he creates, but a large part of the beauty of a Clapton solo is that he's creating it on the fly as he plays. Like all really great improvised solos, Clapton's rise up out of him the way water gushes from a spring – with an almost indescribable energy and vibrancy. That's the product of his soul working on musical raw material he's stockpiled all his life – scales, chords, riffs, rhythms, melodies and harmonies that he's studied and you haven't. Unless you study them, too, you won't be able to do what Clapton does, not really.

The Practicing-Scales-and-Arpeggios-You-Already-Know Approach

The **simplest** way to get better faster is to not only acquire and learn new songs, but also to practice the scales and arpeggios you learned during the Garage Band basics.

I like to think that I'm the average Garage Band graduate, having finished the basics about six months ago. For the past year[1] I've played in a blues band that learns new songs all the time and plays occasional gigs. I play these songs at band practice once a week, but hardly ever practice them at home. Yet, every time I go to band practice, I play the

[1] Written in July 1993

songs better. That's because every day I sit in front of my drum machine and practice my scales and arpeggios a little bit, working through them in different patterns. Six months ago, I could play my blues scales in sixteenth notes at 64 beats per minute. Now I can play most of them at 90 beats per minute. Which means that when I play with the band, my fingers are more confident because they know where to go when they hear the call.

My current goal is to play all the scales I know in rhythm at what I consider a fast pace – maybe 120 beats per minute. Just to put that in perspective, speed-of-light guys like Charlie Parker and Dizzy Gillespie often played at more than 300 beats per minute. (When they get that fast, however, it's mostly eighth notes.)

When I achieve my goal of 120 beats per minute, I will be a much better blues player. I will, as a matter of fact, be smoking. There's only one problem: Even when I accomplish my goal, I still won't play blues like the sax players I admire most, namely Eddie "Lockjaw" Davis, Coleman Hawkins, Stan Getz and Ben Webster. I will hit a ceiling. Why? Because I will still only be able to create the harmonies that can be created with the tools I now possess – namely major and minor blues. I'll have a sharper axe, but it will be the same old axe.

The More-Music-Theory Approach

As we said earlier, the reason Eric Clapton can create what he creates in a solo is that he has lots of musical knowledge stored up in his brain and body. Jazz virtuosos like George Benson and Wynton Marsalis have even more.

Think of a musician's brain and body as a computer. When you buy a computer, it usually has only one program loaded in the memory – an operating system. You really can't do any work with the computer until you buy and load some other programs. If you want to type letters, you buy word-processing software. If you want to keep your company books, you buy an accounting program. Then you can type letters and keep accounts, but you can't lay out a newsletter. To do that, you have to buy and load some desktop-publishing software. Then, if you want to send your newsletter copy to the printer via telephone lines, you have to buy communications software. The list goes on and on and on.

Before you started Garage Band music, you were like a new computer loaded with only an operating system. Completing the Garage Band basics will load a couple of powerful music programs into your hard drive – major and straight blues. As you learn how to use those programs effectively, you may start feeling their limitations. Your computer will still have lots of unused capacity, and you may want to use it. You may want to load more programs.

The way you load them is by learning and practicing additional scales, scale patterns and chords – applied music theory.

Music Theory for Improvised Music

There are two basic musical routes you can choose at the theory junction. One is the route of improvised music, which includes such things as rock, jazz, country, blue grass, reggae and folk music of all countries. The other route is "written" music. The latter includes such work as classical music, big-band arrangements, marching music and so forth.

If you want to play rock, country, blues, reggae or one of the other simple types of improvised music, you should first think about where you want to end up. If your goal is to play at the level of your average bar band (nothing to sneeze at), you should just learn songs and seek out the counsel of people who play the kind of music you like.

If you want to do more, you don't necessarily **have to** study music theory, but it will improve your chances of achieving your own special sound. That's because applied music theory systematizes and compresses what all the great self-taught people learned intuitively in bits and pieces as they traveled through lives focused primarily on music. Music theory as applied to making improvised music is not a complex concept. It simply means learning: 1) more scales and chords; 2) the relationships between the two; and 3) how to use both in the kind of tunes you want to play. Most of the simpler forms of improvised music as performed by most players utilize a limited repertoire of scales and chords. Rock and blues, for example, stick primarily to blues and major scales, but use minor scales a lot of the time. Country sticks mostly to major scales, but also uses blues and minor scales. Irish and English folk music use major scales, but rely heavily on pentatonic scales.

Only one group of improvisers consistently utilizes every scale and chord – bebop jazz players. As a group, jazz players also tend to be more aware of how they use various scales and chords. Rock, blues, reggae and country musicians are more likely to play intuitively. Jazz musicians (especially bebop players) are more likely to analyze and intellectualize what they're doing. That is to say, they not only do it, but can explain it, too.

That's why we arrive at our bottom line advice on applied music theory. If you want to develop your own sound in any kind of improvised music, here's the fastest and surest method:

1. Study and play the **type** of music you like (rock, reggae, country, etc.) with your friends and a teacher who plays that style of music.
2. Study applied music theory (scales, chords, their relations, etc.) with a knowledgeable and articulate bebop jazzer. He or she can not only teach you what most rock, country or reggae people do intuitively, but also will introduce you to all the other musical tools you will use to create you own special sound.

One warning if you take our advice: As you study music theory with your jazz person, keep your attention focused on applying what he or she teaches to the rock, reggae, blues, etc. you want to play. Otherwise, your teacher may lure you into the jazz jungle, never to return.

"Written" Music

Your other alternative is what we call "written music." We put quotation marks around the term because we don't mean just any music that is written down. Almost all types of music are written down these days to make them more accessible. You can buy the melodies and transcribed solos of countless rock, jazz, salsa, African, country, and ... (you name it) ... stars. However, what you're usually buying is something that somebody somewhere improvised. If you go hear them play, they probably won't play it the way it's written.

When we talk about "written" music here, we're talking about music that is meant to be played the same way every time. Classical music is the most obvious example. Big-band jazz arrangements are another. Marching music is another. The music usually is complex, may have multiple parts for various instruments and, according to tradition, is played precisely as written – with the emphasis on *precisely*. Obviously, the approach to this kind of music is different than the approach to improvised music. So, if you choose to pursue this route after you complete the Garage Band basics, you will have to take what amounts to a sharp right turn in your musical career.

The first thing to do is find yourself a good traditional classical teacher who plays the type of music you want to play. The second thing to do is follow his or her instructions. At this point we will abandon you to their care and feeding, since they're into and good at something we're not into.

Most likely they will ask you to "start over" with one of the traditional methods described in the chapter on traditional methods. You have to start from the beginning 1) because you obviously will have to learn to read well to play written music; and 2) because technique for playing written music is different.

You won't really be starting over, because you'll already be a musician. You'll just be learning a different way to play. You will move much more quickly through the classical training than a real beginner because:

1. You are thoroughly familiar with your instrument.
2. You know and can use the major scales and chords of all keys.
3. You know the value and results to be obtained from practice.
4. You know a lot "about" music.
5. Your ear is much more developed than that of a rank novice.
6. You have a lot of musical confidence.

Most important, you're not likely to quit – as so often happens with real beginners learning classical technique. As we said, you'll already be a musician. You'll just want to learn to play in a new and different way.

Style

Style, the third area of advanced study, is not as easy to define as technique and music theory. It's kind of like art; we know it when we see it. A player can have great technique, yet never touch your emotions. That's why we hear people say things like: "She's a fine technician, but she leaves me cold..." On the other hand, you also hear people say, "He's not a great musician, but he's got heart." Most of us would prefer to listen to the latter kind of player.

Style also differentiates good players from one another. Albert King and Stevie Ray Vaughn played similar tunes, but when somebody cues up an Albert King recording you would never mistake it for something by Stevie Ray. Why? What's the difference in their playing? More important, how do you learn to create that difference in your own music? How do you create your own style?

In a little book called *The Sacred Wood*, poet T.S. Eliot observed that art expands upon the tradition from which it flows. First, the artist must learn all there is to know about the art he loves. Then, he or she takes that art one step further. Rarely does work of lasting value spring full blown from the mind of the creator. You can't just do your own thing. Art is an extension of all that came before.

You should approach musical style in the same way. The goal may be to give wings to your own heart and soul, but the way to accomplish that goal is to try to capture the heart and soul of the players who move you. Listen to the music you like. Think about why you like it. Think about how it relates to the man, woman, girl or boy inside you. Listen hard to the music of your favorite stars and identify the nuances that touch you. You want to learn the techniques they use to create those nuances.

You may notice that in the paragraph above we used the word "try." ("... try to capture the heart and soul of the players who move you.") We use that word because trying is what gets you where you really want to be – to a style of your own. You may never capture the off-center rhythm of Thelonius Monk, but if you work at it long enough you will find a compromise that suits your own abilities and feel. You'll sound like you, but people will say, "Hey, I hear some Monk in there somewhere."

Unfortunately, you won't find even the compromises overnight. Style takes time. It comes in bits and pieces over the months and years. Our advice is to take what we think of as a Zen approach. Try, but don't try too hard. First, understand what you value in music. Listen to your favorite players a lot. Always keep them in mind. Have a vision of where you want to end up, and keep that vision in front of you when you play. Don't work at an abstract concept like style. Work at something concrete – how you want to sound. Gradually, you will find yourself becoming more and more like what you have imagined.

Which is not to say that you should simply trust the inevitable flow of history to get you where you want to go. You must always be seeking. When you listen to your favorite players, you will hear the little tricks that make up their style. Over time, you will learn to perform many of these tricks, but some will stump you. If the trick is on a recording, get a friend or teacher to listen with you and figure out what's going on. If you hear the technique live, then go up to the stage at break time and ask the player how he or she did it.

Sometimes that person will be able to tell you what he is doing. Other times, he won't. He'll think a moment, then try to explain how to hold your lips or hands or whatever. When he sees the blank look in your eyes, he'll stop and think again. Finally, though, he may just give up and say, "Hell, I don't know. I just do it."

What we're trying to say is that style is one part of music you have to find yourself – and you will. As you build your chops and your confidence, keep your mind's eye and ear on your vision of the music you want to make. You'll gradually begin to do the musical things your heart wants to do. Trust us. It happens.

Before we end the current discussion, we have to issue one little warning: As you develop your own style, it will inevitably reflect who you are. The more you play, the more your music will lay bare. The common belief is that one creates best when one opens one's soul. We subscribe to that theory. When music works best, it strips back the insulation from the emotional wires of both player and listener; the wires

Chops: *Here's a great musician word you should know. In the broadest sense, it means any musician's technical ability at the moment, as in "How are your chops?" Chops go up or down depending how much the musician has been playing and practicing. In a narrower sense, the term refers to the condition of a horn player's embouchure, i.e., the connection between his or her mouth and the mouthpiece.*

touch, and energy flows – both ways.

You can make your music pop at that level by working hard, playing with people you like and being honest. If you don't work hard, aren't honest or play with bums, you may never strip the insulation from your emotional wiring, but you still will reveal much to your audiences. If you're jammed up and can't plumb the depths of your emotions, your music will reveal your jammed-upness. If you're shallow (and have no depth), your music will reveal that. If you try to please others instead of yourself, your music will show that, too.

So stand forewarned. We're talking emotional sodium pentathol. Be honest and open from the start. You can't lie with music.

Reading Music

After putting the craft of reading music at the bottom of the priority list for a year, we're ready to bring it up somewhere near the middle. Heretofore, we've focussed on other skills. Now we want you to learn to read. If you don't, you may never open a lot of musical doors.

Reading music is just another tool, but it's a powerful one. You can't play in a big band or orchestra without reading. You'll also have a hard time learning a lot of the world's best music if don't read. Worse, you'll waste way too much time struggling over the songs and musical ideas you do learn, most of which will be made easier if you know how to read.

Once you've gone through the Garage Band basics, you'll know how to read at the *Dick and Jane* level. You'll find it frustrating that you don't read better. You'll want to read more complicated stuff, and you'll be poised to do it because you will have learned the scales in all 12 keys by ear. You'll know the spoken language. Now you can go about mastering the written language at a faster and more pleasant pace than if you had put too much emphasis on reading as you learned the basics of your instrument.

Of course, reading well requires discipline and methodical study, even for a Garage Band graduate. We sternly recommend you not try to learn haphazardly by simply reading and mastering songs you like. That tempting path is likely to lead you into the land of the mediocre reader. The goal when reading music is to use your eyes as a scanner that picks up signals and sends them directly to the fingers and other body parts that play the notes. This skill is best learned in systematic increments. Don't waste time trying to reinvent the learning method yourself. There are lots of good books designed to train good readers. Find a teacher to guide you through one of those books or a course of his or her own. Short of that, get a good book yourself and work straight through it. In the end, you'll be glad you did.

Remember, This is a Lifetime Sport

Keep in mind that music is no different than any sport you can play for a lifetime. If you play a few rounds of golf and take it seriously, you become a golfer. As often as you can, you and your friends go out to the golf course and immerse yourselves in a game whose infinite complexities will never cease to fascinate and, sometimes, frustrate you.

You can do the same thing with tennis, fishing, bowling, gardening, mountain biking, running or music. The secret of real success is achieving the level of ability that makes you feel like a golfer, tennis player, fisherman, bowler, gardener, mountain biker, runner or musician. That's the purpose of this book, to bring you to that much desired plateau. Once you get there, you'll be able to figure out what to do.

14

HOW TO FIND THE RIGHT TEACHER

Much of your success as a musician will depend on how well you shop for a teacher. We wish you could open the Yellow Pages, look up Garage Band Music and call a studio full of board-certified masters dedicated to the teaching of our method on any and all instruments. Sad to say, that's not the case. We don't have the resources to start a Garage Band revolution from the top down by building an empire of Garage Band franchises around the country.

Instead, we're looking to start our revolution from the bottom up. We hope to do that by convincing you the method works and persuading you to go out, find a competent teacher and hire him or her to teach you, using the approach outlined in this book, even if he or she has never heard of this book, the Garage Band approach, or us.

It may sound cocky to presume that teachers will embrace our method, but it's really not. Musicians capable of teaching our method are all more or less familiar with the basic elements of it. They have to be. This method is part of what every "complete" musician goes through to become complete. Also, most musicians have at least one thing in common — poverty. If you're willing and able to pay, they will teach you any way you like.

The Ideal Teacher

How do you find a person who can teach you the Garage Band way? Look for the following qualities:

- The ideal teacher is, above all else, a player. Surprisingly, many teachers no longer play much themselves. They're burned out. Steer clear of them.
- The ideal teacher not only plays, he or she is a "complete" musician, proficient at improvising jazz, blues and rock as well as reading music. (As we've said before, many fine classical musicians can read like the dickens, but don't improvise well. They make fine classical teachers, but if they don't improvise, they're not equipped to teach you blues, rock, country, reggae, jazz, etc. — all of which are improvised, not read.)
- The ideal teacher has a broad knowledge of music theory, i.e. knows not only how to play, but also why things fit together as they do.
- The ideal teacher not only has lots of knowledge and skills, but also knows how to communicate them to you.
- The ideal teacher is able to establish a warm rapport with you.
- The ideal teacher is not too serious; he or she knows your goal is to have fun.
- The ideal teacher loves making music and radiates that joy.
- The ideal teacher knows how to instill and inspire confidence in you, making you believe you will achieve whatever goal you set for yourself.
- The ideal teacher inspires awe in his or her abilities, too, convincing you that he or she is a wise master, worthy not only of your respect, but also of the time and money you will invest in the endeavor.

The character we've just described may sound too Godlike to be true, but isn't. Bob has all these qualities and he's not remotely Godlike, just an average decent guy who knows a lot about music. Every city of any size has musicians just like him. Our hometown, Boise, population 125,000, has 20 to 25 that we know of.

Of course, Boise has a lot more than 25 people teaching private music lessons. The problem is sorting out the ones who can deliver what you want. First, of course, you have to identify all the people who teach your particular instrument. You do that by asking around. Ask at all the local music stores; they usually have a crew of teachers who give private lessons in studios in the store. Go to clubs and find people who play the music you want to play. Ask them if they give lessons or know someone who can teach you. Most of the good musicians in town know each other. Call up high school and college band directors. Find out who gives private lessons to band members — particularly their best ones. Other sources to check are church music directors, leaders of community bands and orchestras, music societies, etc. If you live in a reasonably big town, you no doubt will identify several potential teachers — lots if you want to play guitar or piano, fewer for other instruments.

Interrogating the Prospective Teacher

Then comes the hard part, winnowing out the chaff. We suggest you do this by asking each of the prospective teachers the following questions. They will help you identify a teacher who can turn you into the kind of recreational musician we've described in this book.

Do you improvise?

The answer you seek is a strong, "Yes." Be leery of anyone who hems, haws and/or looks in any way suspicious when they tell you they can improvise. Many musicians hate to admit they can't. You've got to find out. This method should be taught only by those who are accomplished improvisers, at least in blues, rock or country, preferably in jazz.

Do you play blues?

Again, you're looking for a strong yes. The method is based on the blues. You don't want a teacher who's never played them.

Do you read music?

Varying levels of reading are acceptable if the teacher is accomplished in other ways. If you have a choice, you don't want to take lessons from a person who doesn't read at all. Many fine players don't read, but the best teachers read well.

What types of music do you play?

This is not a make-or-break question, but can help you differentiate the good from the great. The best combination is an accomplished jazz player who also likes the kind of music you like. As we've said before, a good jazz player is likely to possess more musical knowledge and improvising ability than anyone else. However, another big consideration is the teacher's passion for the kind of music you love. If you lust after country and have the choice between a great country player and a jazz snob who hates country, then go with your soul mate.

What's your training?

The question of whether a person is self-taught, attended a university or took years of private lessons is another guide to ability. Sometimes the meaning is obvious. If they studied jazz at Eastman, Berklee, North Texas or one of the other great music programs, you've probably found a gold mine. Formal training not only means more formal knowledge, but lots of exposure to teachers and teaching techniques, which can translate into teaching ability. You must, of course, balance this kind of training against real-world experience. (See next question.)

The Teacher Will be your Employee

When you interview a prospective teacher, remember what you're trying to do: use your hard-earned money to hire a person to work for you. Don't be intimidated. Make sure you hire someone who can deliver.

How much do you play and where?

You often, though not always, can judge the caliber of a musician by his or her gigs. This rule, unfortunately, has lots of exceptions. It's not always the best players who get the best jobs. The test is better if you ask who the teacher plays with in addition to where. Bad musicians sometimes play well-paying gigs, but usually don't play with really good players.

How much teaching have you done?

Teaching experience is not essential. However, if a player has taught a lot, he or she probably has learned a good deal about how people learn. That's a definite advantage.

Do you understand and teach jazz, blues and/or rock theory?

An understanding of jazz theory is valuable, but not essential. The theory used in jazz is a more comprehensive version of the theory used in blues, rock, country and other improvised popular music, which the teacher **must** understand, use and be able to teach. A jazz theorist simply can take you further along any improvising path you choose to follow. Be aware that jazz-blues-rock theory is different from classical theory. A teacher can be well-versed in the classical approach and yet not have a working knowledge of even rock or blues, let alone jazz.

Play something for me.

This is an important test. Ideally, you want to take lessons from somebody whose music knocks you out. If it doesn't, beware.

How are your students doing?

This is not a make-or-break question, either, because it is so tough to analyze. There are lots of "classical-approach' teachers who have very successful students, but to our way of thinking aren't the kind of teacher you want. Usually, their success stories are brilliant kids. The teacher turns them into great readers, hones their technique and instills a love of music. Lots of teachers can do that with the few kids who have the talent and discipline to generate themselves ample rewards as they struggle through a classical regime. A teacher may send all his or her graduates off to Julliard, but it doesn't necessarily follow that he or she will be a good teacher for you. What you really want to hear is that all the teacher's students are playing music with their friends and having the time of their lives. That's the real test.

Don't Be Passive

When you finally choose a teacher, you have to take responsibility for success on yourself. Don't sit passively by taking orders and expecting the teacher to mold you into a great player. You have to communicate with a teacher. At the start, you have to make sure he or she understands exactly what you want to learn and where you want to end up. Later on, you have to make sure the teacher knows what's going on with your playing. He or she may only hear you play a half hour a week. During that half hour, you have to make sure you communicate what's going right and wrong, so the teacher can keep doing the right stuff and get to work on the wrong stuff.

If It Doesn't Work Out

If you take lessons from somebody and practice hard, but feel like you aren't making enough progress after a few weeks, be blunt. Tell the teacher about your concerns. If things don't improve, find another teacher. Whatever you do, don't assume that you lack what it takes to play music. If you're willing to put in the practice time, you can do this. I tried a half-dozen teachers over a period of 30 years before I found the right one. Six months later, I was playing in a blues band. Keep looking for the right person to guide your steps. Good teachers are not always easy to find, but if you follow the steps we've outlined, the search shouldn't take 30 years, either.

15

OTHER INSTRUMENTS

We could provide a detailed explanation of how to approach every instrument for which this method is appropriate, but we hope that by now you've gotten the idea. The key to the Garage Band method is that you can find an easy way to groove on most popular instruments, just as we've illustrated with the sax, guitar and piano. Moreover, you can learn that easy way to groove in a relatively short time. So, you can begin playing real music along with a real rhythm section from almost the beginning of your musical instruction – on nearly any instrument you might want to play.

It would be a misleading, of course, to tell you that every instrument is as easy to learn as every other or that our approach is as straightforward and practical for every instrument as it is for the sax, piano and guitar. In the following pages, we've tried to provide an honest appraisal of how our blues-based method will apply to the various families of instruments.

Flutes and Single Reed Instruments (Such as Clarinet)

Flutes and the clarinets can be learned through the Garage Band method in the same manner as the saxophone. That's because they're fingered in a similar way and require a similar level of physical training to get satisfactory tones from the instrument. If you follow the routine laid out for the sax, you will learn the flute or clarinet at about the same rate of speed as the novice saxophonist, although getting a good tone on a flute or clarinet presents different problems. The clarinet, for example, requires a good deal more strength in the embouchure and the diaphragm because you have to push air through a smaller, more resistant tube. The trade-off is that a clarinet is easier to play in tune than a sax.

One other difficulty with clarinets and flutes is that fewer people are playing blues on these instruments these days, so you'll have to look harder to find a tradition to draw from. You'll find some blues among the work of jazz guys like flute players Herbie Mann and Frank Wess and clarinetists Pete Fountain and Eddie Daniels, but you'll have to look to saxophonists, guitarists and masters of other hard-core blues instruments if you want to find a variety of simple, easy-to-learn musical ideas.

Double Reed Instruments

If you're so bold as to try to play blues on the more exotic, double reed instruments such as oboe and bassoon – which we think would be great – you, too, can use the sax method, but no doubt will find the going slower. The double reeds are physically demanding because you have to push an airstream through a tiny tube and control not one, but two, reeds. There's no way around the strenous training requirements that have made oboists and bassonists a rare breed. Moreover, you'll have *nowhere* to turn for tradition, because the great double reed players just don't seem to dabble in blues, at least not so far as we can tell. (Although once this book is widely published, we're certain to receive at least one letter cluing us to some wonderfully obscure blues oboist.) You also will have a hard time finding a teacher who improvises. One place you might want to start is by contacting Music for People, a nationwide group that promotes improvising and has a classical leaning. Its address is listed in *Chapter 18: Other Books, CDs, Videos, Etc.*

In any case, don't let us discourage you. If you played oboe as a kid in high school orchestra and are rekindling your love of music, go for the gold. The music of the double reeds is among the most beautiful in the world. We'd like nothing better than to find out we inspired a few people to play blues on them. It's a niche waiting to be filled.

Bass

If you want to play music with people as quickly as possible, consider the bass. It's simple to learn, and bassists are in great demand.

The function of the bass is to lay down the rhythmic groove and the bottom of the chord progression. The bassist performs this important task by playing rhythm patterns made up almost exclusively of chord tones, with a primary focus on the root of the chord (meaning he or she plays the root more than the other chord tones.) The principal exception to the use of chord tones is the use of passing tones from an appropriate scale when more-advanced players move from one chord to another through the tune.

So, there are two ways in which the Garage Band method *doesn't* fit the bass. One, bassists don't improvise a lot, so it doesn't make sense to start out improvising on the bass. Two, bassists play mostly chord tones, so it doen't make sense to start out learning blues scales.

Fortunately, the underlying principles of the method do work for the bass, just as for other instruments. You start out by playing a simple groove over a 12-bar blues, but do it with chord tones instead of a blues scale. In fact, we think the best approach for novices is to start with the simplest groove of all – playing the root of the chord on every beat, starting with the root of the I chord, then moving to the root of the IV chord at the appropriate time, then back to the root of the

I chord and so on and so on.

Believe us, this is really easy. And if you can do it with a steady beat, there are plenty of guitar players who'll be glad to have you playing with them in the garage. Moreover, they and / or a teacher will quickly show you how to move on to more challenging grooves. That – learning your chords and standard grooves – is what you'll do on the bass instead of improvising. We also recommend the book *Bass Guitar* by Jim Gregory and Harvey Vinson, which is published by Consolidated Music Publishers and is available in lots of music stores. It uses an approach similar to ours.

The User-Friendly Electric Bass: If you choose to play the electric bass, you'll want to follow the guitar approach, because you'll learn to play the individual notes of a chord on it in the same way a guitarist learns to play the notes of a scale – in patterns or shapes. Once you learn the patterns for the I chord, IV chord and V chord in any key, you'll be able to play 12-bar blues in any other key by simply moving the patterns to other positions on the fret board.

The Stand-Up Bass: The stand-up acoustic bass isn't played like an electric bass or guitar. On a stand-up bass, the chord tones in each key are fingered differently, which means you should follow a routine like that laid our for the sax – learning one new key a month until you have all 12 under your fingers.

Brass Horns (Like Trumpet and Tuba)

One of our dearest wishes is that more tuba players would take up the blues. Performers like Taj Mahal and Leon Redbone have amply illustrated the true elegance of tubists by employing them as bass players. Unfortunately, we feel compelled to point out that our method is more practical for tuba and other brass players who have at least a little junior high or high school experience and want to learn to improvise than it is for complete novices. If you played trumpet or tuba in high school and want to go back to it, this is a great method. Just apply the saxophone approach. It will work fine for you.

Beginners will find our method is not quite so straightfoward for them. You'll recall that the sax approach requires the student to move from key to key, learning at least one octave of the blues scale in each. There's the rub for novice brass players. Because of the nature of the brass instruments, beginners do well to obtain a range of a single octave in the easiest-to-play key. Beginning trumpet players, for example, generally are limited to the range from the C below the staff to the C in the middle of the staff.

C Major Scale

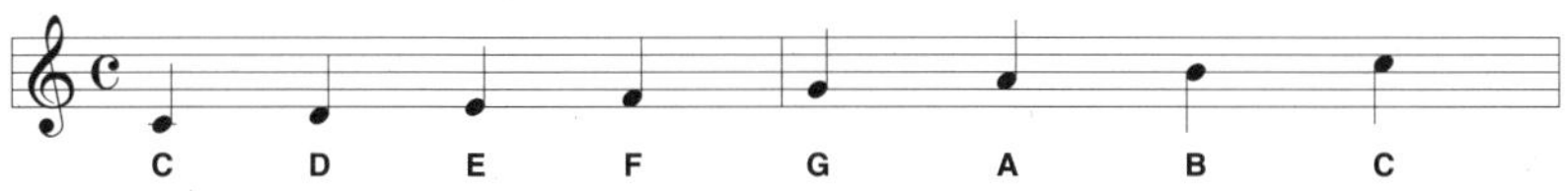

So when a beginning trumpet player learning from a traditional teacher is ready to learn a new major scale, he or she learns it in that range, starting from the root and going up, but dropping down an octave when the scale goes beyond his or her range, as shown in the following diagram for the G major scale.

G Major Scale for Beginning Trumpet

You can do the same thing for blues scales, which is fine for those of you who played and read music in a past life, but may be a little tough for rank beginners.

Drums

We don't have a lot to say about drumming, since it is a different sort of game and, as Bob says, most drummers can't read anyway. (Only kidding.) Our only contribution to this trade is the reminder that the guiding principles of the Garage Band still apply. It's best to start with a simple groove, and the best way to build personal momentum is to play with other people.

Bowed Instruments (Like the Violin)

Where the Garage Band method is concerned, learning to play the bowed instruments is more like learning to play a saxophone than like learning to play a guitar. That's because even though a bowed instrument like a violin looks sort of like a guitar, it has a much shorter neck. That means a violin is not quite so user-friendly as a guitar. You can't just learn the fingering patterns for the I chord, IV chord and V chord in one key, then move the patterns to a different position to play in other keys.

On the violin, you have to learn different fingering patterns for the chords in every key, which means you want to use the saxophone approach if you're going to apply the Garage Band method to the violin or another bowed instrument. Learn to play 12-bar blues in one key a month, and, at the end of a year, you'll have built yourself a solid foundation on the instrument.

The same holds true for the cello. Even though it has a longer neck and theoretically could be played like the guitar (by using the same fingering patterns in different keys), that's not the way cellists do it.

Like violinists and saxophone players, they finger the chords and scales differently in every key. So, use the sax approach.

Players of bowed instruments will have the same problem faced by the players of the more esoteric reed instruments. You'll be hard-pressed to find an improvising teacher or much of a tradition for blues violin, viola or cello. There are some blues fiddlers out there – Papa John Creech is a good example – but they're few and far between. Please, though, don't let that discourage you. When our violinist friend Jazzmo Seiler sits in with our band, he blazes, invariably drawing more applause than anyone else. You may also want to follow our advice to the double reed players – contact Music for People, where you'll find lots of improvising violinists and cellists.

Blues Harp

Reading this book will help you learn to play blues harp by helping you understand how music and the blues work, but our method doesn't really apply to the harp except in basic principles – start with a simple groove and, above all, play with people. Fortunately, there are several really good books on learning to play blues harp. Our favorite is *Blues and Rock Harmonica Made Easy* by David Harp.

16

PLAYING WITH OTHER PEOPLE

If you want to learn to play an instrument, you should begin making music with other people as soon as possible. Don't wait until you are "good enough." Once you've gone through a month or so of the Garage Band basics, you know plenty. Go out, find people with musical interests similar to your own and bring them together for a jam session. You will find that if you put out the energy to organize a jam, you can attract more-accomplished but less-driven musicians who are too lazy to organize their own sessions. People like to make music. They like to show off their talents, too. The only requirement for getting them together is that you let down your inhibitions so you can get over the first and only hurdle – baring your soul to other human beings by asking them if they would like to try to make music with you.

People in the Same Boat as You

When I first started trying to play the sax, part of my work involved producing an illustrated directory for Idaho's colleges and universities. One day in the graphics studio, I overheard a designer named Adele Thomsen talk about playing blues. I didn't know Adele well, so I didn't say anything. I was too shy. That night, I chided myself. I had been acquainted with Adele for a couple of years, if slightly. Why was I afraid to tell her I was trying to learn to play the sax? What did I fear?

Rejection? That she would make fun of me, think I was a fool or laugh in my face? When I examined my shyness, I couldn't really figure out why I had failed to speak up. It didn't make sense. I wanted to know people who played blues. I had been thinking about it for weeks. Yet, when offered a golden opportunity, I passed. I promised myself I would correct my mistake the next time I saw Adele.

When I finally asked about her music a week later, she didn't laugh in my face. She told me she had played banjo for years but recently had started over, playing delta blues guitar – just the kind of music I loved. It seems she wanted to forget her ex-husband and the bluegrass music they'd played together. I told her about my sax playing, going to great lengths to make clear how poorly I played. Would she like to try working up some tunes some evening? If it worked, great. If it didn't, we just wouldn't do it any more.

It worked. Adele and I turned out to be great for each other. I helped her by just showing up every Thursday evening. She needed someone to play and talk music with – even a novice. Thus motivated, she doubled her practice time.

I profited more directly. Adele was a far better musician than I. She knew a couple of dozen songs and sang like Ma Rainey. Most important for me, she knew how to groove. She would crank up the volume on her guitar amp, kick into a song, knock out a couple of verses, then step back and play rhythm while I worked through simple blues riffs, picking them out by ear.

That summer with Adele, I felt like a musician. I was making real live music from thin air. It sounded fine, too. I knew that because after a while one of Adele's neighbors started dropping in to listen. Sometimes when we propped the front door open, we'd see a neighboring gardener linger over her flower beds, listening while she tended her daisies and black-eyed Susans. We were not great. We've both come a long way since, and cringe a little, looking back. But – the neighbors still liked it.

We also began to attract other musicians. A couple of times, a kid from the graphics shop came over to play bass. Once, he brought his mother to hear us play. When Adele's brother came to town, he played Dobro with us. When these people showed up, I was in heaven. Despite my almost non-existent skills on the sax, I had arrived. I played music with people, and others liked to listen.

You can do the same thing. At that time, I could **barely** play the sax. I didn't really have **any** blues scales under my fingers. I could not follow chord changes at all. I had a terrible tone (the first thing Bob told me when I found him later in the year). All I could do was play a few simple riffs, staying in the right key by ear and by my scant knowledge of music theory (far less than you now possess if you have read this far in the book). Yet I could make enjoyable music with other people. Once I realized that, I had so much fun I couldn't believe it.

The Key Element for a Jam

If you want to have a good blues, rock or country jam, you need at least one person like Adele who: a) knows the words and chords to some songs and b) can play the role of rhythm section by keeping the groove going. If you have that foundation, any number of lesser musicians can play along on any instruments capable of creating a tone or banging out a rhythm. However, if you don't yet know a rhythm player, don't let that stop you. If you play sax and your best friend plays flute, then get together and substitute a recorded rhythm section for the live guitarist, bass and drums. Jamming to a recorded rhythm section is even more fun for two people than it is alone.

Where to Find People Like Adele

The way to find other players at your level or somewhat above is simply to start asking around. Talk to anybody you can find who is involved in music in any way, whether playing in a club, working in a music store, giving private lessons or singing folk songs around a campfire. Ask them if they know anybody who might like to get together with you. Accomplished musicians often have friends or students of lesser ability. Teachers are always encouraging their students to find people to jam with.

This, of course, requires to you be aggressive in a way that may make you uncomfortable. It did me. For most of my life, I've wanted to play music, and for most of my life, I've feared musicians. Until the last two years, whenever I walked into a music store I feared talking to the clerks. I knew they were musicians, and I didn't want to reveal myself as an ignoramus who could never possibly learn the things these people knew. Even now, when I know lots of musicians and will even try out saxophones on the floor in strange music stores, I still fall prey to my phobia. You have to overcome that fear.

But **you** never run into **any** musicians, you say? Think hard. If you go to church, you surely do. Churches are full of musicians for some reason, probably because a little voice deep inside keeps telling us we can always depend on music to lead us to the sublime. If you're not into religion, how about the people on your job or at the bar where you go to rest your elbows. Maybe there's someone in your motorcycle gang, weekly poker game, AA meeting or Toastmasters chapter.

Other Places to Find Musicians

If you want quick and certain results, contact people in local musical organizations. You may be surprised at how many there are. In Boise, we have a bluegrass society, a blues society, a classical chorale, a philharmonic, a community band, a chamber music group, a musical theater troupe, a half-dozen music stores, two musical instrument repair shops, a university music department, a barbershop quartet organization, a musical folklore society, a jazz society, square dance clubs and more. All of them involve people who love sharing what they do. All **you** have to do is ask. One of these people will know somebody who's looking for a musical match like you.

Older Players as Mentors

One great source of musical knowledge and friendship is older musicians, particularly people who are retired and have time to share their skills. I owe my new mid-life musical career to my saintly father-in-law, Mr. Ed Brunner, who was my mentor before I met Adele or Bob.

For the last dozen or so years, I've hung out in the circle of Brunner in-laws and out-laws who gather from around the house when Ed sits down at the piano to play from his endless repertoire of tunes popular in the 1940s when he blew tenor sax in dance bands in Colorado and Montana. When I went out and bought a sax myself, Ed offered to get together to read and play tunes out of a fake book – a generous offer considering I played like a sixth-grader in beginning band. He taught me dozens of wonderful old Tin Pan Alley songs like *When My Baby Walks Down the Street* and *Ain't Misbehavin'*. With his tutelage, support and encouragement, I got better. Gradually, I began to feel a little like a musician, even though my skills were minimal.

Great, you say, but all your father-in-law does for relaxation is watch the Green Bay Packers and crush beer cans against his forehead. That's no excuse. Somewhere near you is an older musician who loves to play and will do so with you at the drop of the hat. One of my favorite musical experiences occurred when I took my sax down to California on a long weekend visit to the home of my friend Bill Burnett, a sometime piano player who works as a copy editor for the San Francisco *Examiner*. "You've got to meet Lois, my mom" he said. Shortly thereafter, he drove me to Lois' condo in Oakland, where he deposited me in the living room with her and her grand piano, while he retired to the kitchen to cook lunch. Lois hadn't had anyone to play music with for months. She and I played almost two hours. She was about the same age as my father-in-law – early 70s – and knew all the songs he had taught me. It didn't matter that I'd left my fake book at home. Lois patiently taught me to play songs by ear. We had a ball.

If you want to find an older mentor, you can. They're out there and comprise a great resource because they have time to play and, often, want to share their skills and songs with younger generations. If you don't have older musicians in your family or circle of friends, inquire at music stores, the community band or local senior organizations.

Don't Be Shy

If you're not ready to venture outside your social circle, try this. For two weeks, ask **everybody** you talk to if they play music or know someone who does. Ask your friends and relatives first. When I published a piece about playing music in *Newsweek*, I got calls from at least a half-dozen friends who had been playing for years without my knowledge. One was a sax-playing Statehouse reporter, another a guitar-picking legislator. Another reporter sang in a barber shop quartet. The head of the teachers union played trumpet.

If you can't find players among your friends and extended family, ask your bank teller, grocery checker, favorite cocktail waitress, mailman, masseuse, bookmaker, etc. Just talk to people. Tell them what you're looking for and why. People like to help. If the ones you ask don't play, one of them will direct you to someone else who does.

A tactical suggestion: When you suggest getting together to play with someone, be self-effacing. Try to make clear to them the skill level at which you play so they can make up their minds about whether they'll have fun with you. Also make clear that you won't be offended if, after one session, they decide the relationship with you isn't going to work out.

Don't make up their minds for them by telling them they're too good to play with you. Be sensible, of course. If you're just starting out, don't try to arrange a jam with the pianist at the best jazz club in town. On the other hand, you should never assume that players who seem more accomplished won't be bothered with you. Some time back, I invited a piano student friend to jam with our band. He never accepted; I'm not sure why. Maybe it was because he didn't have time or didn't care to hang out with us, but I'm afraid that he felt intimidated. If that's the case, it's unfortunate, because we were and remain – how should I say it in the kindest possible way – unpolished? He could easily have kept pace with us. His reluctance was our loss.

Anyway, if someone asks, they generally want you to accept. There are plenty of reasons that players who seem "better" will want you to join them. Maybe they just don't have anybody else to play with. Maybe they're really not that much better. Maybe they like to nurture beginners. Maybe it builds their egos. Maybe they need a piano player and see your potential to improve quickly. Maybe they always wanted to have a little brother or sister to boss around.

Whatever the reasons, you will find that if you consistently take the initiative to ask, you'll end up playing a lot of the time with more accomplished musicians, which is a situation much to be desired. They teach you things you want to know.

What to Do When Someone Says Yes

When you finally run into someone who lights up at the suggestion that the two of you make some music, don't say, "Let's get together some time." Instead, ask: "When are you free this week?"

Financial advisers like to tell people that the most important factor in investing is not where you put your money, but when you start socking it away. The sooner you start, the sooner you'll be able to retire to a tropical isle. The same holds true for playing music. Don't wait. Make a date and get started.

What you do when the two of you meet for the first time depends on your skill levels, musical tastes and the instruments you play. Suppose you both are beginning guitar players; you each know a few chords, but not much else. Since you personally have been studying the Garage Band method for six weeks, you know the 12-bar blues form in the key of A, so that's probably where you want to start. You teach your new friend the chords in A (if he doesn't know them already) and how they change through the form. Then you pick a rhythm for your strum and set up a groove on the A blues form, playing through it in unison. The fact that you've chosen to play the guitar probably means you like to sing, too. As a Garage Band student, you know that you can sing the words of any 12-bar blues with the A groove you've just set up, so that's what you and your buddy do, jumping right into *Ain't Nothing But a Hound Dog,* since it's a tune you both know. After you try that a few times, your pal says he knows the words to *Sweet Home Chicago* and asks if it's a 12-bar tune. You're not sure, but try it out on the chord progression. Sure enough, it is, so you do it.

Your first-jam scenario will go differently if one or both of you is more experienced and knows the form for some different songs. In that case, you may want to start off teaching each other the chords and words to those tunes. Even so, it's still a good idea to learn the words and melodies to 12-bar blues tunes and work on your ability to play the 12-bar form in several keys. This is an easy way to build up your repertoire quickly. It will prove particularly valuable when you invite other musicians to your jams, because the new players will be able to swing right into the 12-bar tunes without any coaching from you.

Of course, this first-jam scenario will go much differently if the two of you play horns instead of guitars. It's difficult for two novice horn players to set up a groove by themselves. What you'll probably want to do is play along with a recorded rhythm section like that on the Garage Band CD. If you're more advanced or want greater variety, you can find lots of play-along material in the Jamey Aebersold Music Co. catalogue, which you can get by calling (800) 456-1388, by fax at (812) 949-2006 or by mail at P.O. Box 1244C, New Albany, IN 474151-1244.

We personally feel the ideal novice get-together is for one of you to play a solo instrument, such as a horn or violin, and the other to be a guitarist or piano player, i.e., to be able play either solo or rhythm. One of our big goals in life is to get these kinds of players to join forces. One of the great failures of musical training in our culture is that horn and reed players from the marching band, string players from the orchestra, drummers and guitar players from the garage, and pianists – who learn from private teachers – seldom share what they know. As a group, guitarists are the only ones good at forming musical liaisons with their friends. Even they usually fail to realize that a piano, horn or violin could double or triple the musical interest of their band.

The combination of a solo instrument and rhythm instrument is our favorite for a first-time jam because it forms the seed for a full-fledged, all-purpose, can-do band. If you're a part of such a jam, you'll start out much like the two fledgling guitarists we described earlier.

Suppose you and your pal play sax and guitar. You have a whole host of musical options and sounds you can explore.

- You can play 12-bar blues or whatever simple two- and three-chord songs one or both of you know.
- The guitarist can sing.
- The guitarist can improvise solos.
- The saxophonist can play "fills" behind the guitarist's singing, i.e., blowing simple blues scale riffs at the end of phrases.
- The saxophonist can play the melody or improvise while the guitarist plays rhythm.
- When the saxophonist isn't playing, he or she can sing or play a percussion instrument like a guiro or tambourine.

Given all these possibilities, the two of you can create a whole houseful of music. The only duty that must be performed is that of the guitarist to play rhythm, which forms the foundation for whatever else you do.

First Gig – The Best Way to Learn

Once you and your new friend confirm that you can have fun playing music in your garage, you no doubt will experience one of two common urges. You'll either want to find some more players and form a band or you'll love the way the two of you sound together, in which case you will want to work up some tunes to play for other people – a performance.

If you're immediately happy with the new musical relationship you've created, we urge you to follow the natural desire to find yourself a gig – any gig. My fiddle-playing barber, Al, gave me that advice when I could hardly play a lick: "If you want to get better fast," he said, "pick out some tunes and schedule a performance." I'm proud to say I followed his sage counsel, and it works.

You don't have to book Carnegie Hall. If you're just starting out, you'll probably want to pick your audience carefully – sticking to friends and/or relatives you know will get into and enjoy what you do. Our band performed for the first time at a Blues Society jam session. The situation was ideal. On one hand, we felt comfortable because we knew most of the people in the audience would be friends who liked us, liked the kind of music we played, knew we were novices and wanted to nurture us along because most of them were amateur musicians, too. They either had the same fears as us or remembered having them. On the other hand, the society held the jam at a local bar with a real stage and regular paying customers sprinkled among our friends. That reality was just intimidating enough to make us get our act together.

Once we decided to play the jam and imagined ourselves on that stage, we got serious about our tunes in a way we never had before. We picked our five best songs and focussed on perfecting them. Tinged with an edge of pleasurable anxiety, our rehearsals got more organized. We started arranging beginnings and endings for tunes instead of just fading (stumbling?) in and out of them. We each practiced more at home. The two vocalists got their words down. We scheduled extra rehearsals. We worked.

The week before the jam, our excitement began to rise and our anxiety to fade – because we realized how much we had improved. We had a blast at our last practice, because all of a sudden we sounded a lot better than we had the week before.

Buoyed by a new confidence, we cooked at the jam. We entertained people – not because we were the best band they'd ever heard, but because we worked at our music, put our hearts into it and exceeded our own expectations, having fun and generating a warm, fuzzy glow of positive energy.

The Band

Of course, you and your pal may not be ready for a performance yet. Maybe you want the camaraderie of a larger group. Or maybe you're not satisfied with your duo. Maybe you and your first partner are not a perfect fit. Jerry Garcia once said that it's easy to find players; there are plenty hanging out at the music store. The hard part is finding people you want to spend time around.

My musical relationship with Adele broke up after a few months for musical reasons. Being a duo was hard work for Adele. Singing, playing rhythm and working in smooth solos all by yourself requires serious concentration. Pretty soon we began to think about how nice it would be to have a bass player or another guitarist to keep that nice steady groove going. Then there was the problem of our dynamics. A tenor sax and acoustic guitar are not a match made in heaven, though like any combination of musical instruments they can work together if you want them to and have access to amplification.

We basically had three instruments – my sax, Adele's amplified Martin flat-top and her voice. A saxophone in the hands of a novice is not a subtle instrument. Playing quietly is a skill that takes time to develop. I sounded best when I played loudly, so I did. That created problems for Adele. Even singing through a mike, she pushed her voice to match the sax. Consequently, we struggled to accommodate each other. I even went so far as to stuff a sock in the bell of my horn.

The final solution appeared when Adele ran into a bass player who wanted to start a band. The problem was, I didn't fit into the picture. The first time Adele told me about this great guy, Larry, I saw the freight train heading toward our musical relationship. When I asked why she hadn't invited him to come play with us, she got a little nervous look on her face that set off simultaneous flashbacks in my mind of a girl and two women who had broken my heart at various points in the past. Adele and I were just pals, but she betrayed the tell-tale body language of a kind-hearted woman about to let a good man down easy.

I figured it would take her two, maybe three weeks to actually come across with the bad news. My feelings hurt a little at first, but I figured she might be right about it being time for us to move on. (The girl and two women in my flashbacks had all been right.)

I should have told her that I got the picture and bowed out gracefully. Instead, I took a slightly sadistic pleasure in the next three weeks of soap opera, innocently asking about Larry every chance I got, then watching Adele agonize over whether to admit she had been playing with him on the side. During a break in a practice session three weeks later, she steeled herself and broke the news. I, of course, gave her no end of guff about dumping me for another guy. We laughed and remained friends. She had made a good call. We both went on to new stages of development, even though her musical fling with Larry didn't work into a band.

The Formation of Bands

Bands, like most of life, usually do not come off according to plan. It's tempting to say they just happen, but that's not true, either. The essential ingredient is somebody who wants a band badly enough to put the pieces together. Dennis, the vocalist and harmonica player in our band, provided the spark for the band I play in now. He had played in blues bands during his twenties and decided to get another one going. He had his eye on a guitar player, Ron Stacy, a mellow fellow who ran a mountain-bike shop and hung out with some of Dennis' fellow firefighters. When Dennis heard about the Boise Blues Society jam, he showed up to play and scout for other players who might fit in with him and Ron. That's where he heard me play sax and Mike Rogers – a jeweler – play guitar. He liked Mike because Mike played well. He liked me because I was the only saxophonist there and sounded like I might learn to play if given the chance. He suggested we hold a jam.

The four of us played together for six months before we found a regular drummer – an editor at the newspaper where I used to work. We never could find a regular bass player, so I talked Bob – my co-author and sax teacher – into learning to play bass. We then had all the makings of a band.

As a novice reading this book to figure out whether and how you may learn to play music, you probably wonder why we're going on at such length about starting a band. You no doubt have a hard time imagining yourself playing at all, let alone playing with others on a stage in a bar or at a dance. We're talking about bands because we **want** you to play in a band – because that's the best way to learn.

If you try to play, you should and probably will start fantasizing about a band. This fantasy creeps up from behind you. I assure you I had no delusions of grandeur when I started playing the sax. I knew several fine musicians and how hard they had struggled to achieve even small successes. Yet I remember clearly how I felt after my first great stroke from a stranger. I wasn't even performing. I was practicing every evening in the living room of our little house in Boise's North End, which sits near the sidewalk so any passerby can hear me playing. On Halloween, a couple of months after we moved into the house, a young woman from around the block brought her two kids to trick or treat. "By the way," she said, "I love your saxophone playing. It's beautiful."

After they left, I unwrapped myself a Snickers from the candy bowl, sat on the sofa and enjoyed the waves of satisfaction that flowed over me. Maybe I did have what it took, I thought. Maybe I could be a terrific sax player. Maybe I'd break all the rules. Maybe I would succeed at my quest, whatever it was. Visions of MTV and Carnegie Hall tripped lightly through my imagination, no longer bound by the laws of time, space or common sense. I knew I was a terrible player; at that time, I had not even met Bob. Yet – an obviously intelligent and sensitive human being capable of rearing two healthy children had praised my music. She must have heard a spark of something valuable. If that spark existed, might I not nurture it into a warm flame?

The Development of a Band

Of course, living out that fantasy by forming a band is not all sweetness, light and basking in the praise of strangers. You may struggle, for example, to find a place you can practice. For six months, our jam session moved from house to house, working around the schedules of spouses who liked the idea of a band but turned frosty when asked to bless two to four hours of way-loud blues in their living room or garage. Eventually, you find the tolerant spouse or roommate who lets you make her house your home. That happened to us when we recruited our drummer, Pat. His wife, Suzy, actually enjoys having us practice every week in her family room.

Next, you struggle with the question of **when** to practice. For six months we played round robin on the telephone each week, trying to figure out which evening or afternoon we could all get free **and** find a place to play. Not until Suzy adopted us did we realize we could solve this problem by practicing at the same time every week. Your basic rocket science.

Right about then, the band members start getting irritated by conflicts over what songs to play. Like other bands, we discovered that the members of the rhythm section most often get to say yea or nay to songs proposed by other members of the band. This had proved most irritating to Dennis, our lead singer, who couldn't understand why the guitar players failed to learn the new songs that Dennis taped and brought to practice. The reason they didn't, of course, is that listening to a song and pulling the chord changes, riffs, etc. requires work at home. Since guitarists Ron and Mike had limited time to practice, they worked on the songs they really liked.

Part one of the eventual solution was for Dennis to start bringing in more songs. Ron and Mike were bound to like some of them. Part two was for Dennis to figure out in advance what Ron and Mike would like. Part three was for Dennis to start grumbling in a friendly way about songs he didn't like – so they'd get thrown out. That's the natural process, the way band members focus on the overlap between their musical tastes. As they do so, they develop a sound based on their unique mix of people and experiences. If the mix is right, you become the Grateful Dead or ZZ Top. If not, and you stick together, you eventually may get well-acquainted with the lounge at the Holiday Inn.

As you go through this process of bickering over what songs to play, your first gig will appear. They really do just "appear." Ours came from a friend. He had been asked to provide music for a gathering of a local environmental group. He couldn't do it, so he suggested us. Bob's dad booked Bob's first gig when Bob was 15 – playing for dad's company office party at the poshest restaurant in town. Bob's jazz quartet knew seven tunes, which they played over and over again for three hours. The band members each earned $14 in tips. That was better than our band did; we played free.

Once you book your first gig, you'll start arguing about a band name – a debate that will continue for months because at least half of the band will hate the first, second, third and maybe more of the names you go through. We started out as the Very Shy Blues Band, which half of us hated. Then we became the Hardtones, which half of us hated. As I write, we're Men in Shorts, which half of us hate.

On the heels of your first gig, somebody will suggest you buy a p.a.

system – the microphones, amplifier and speakers used by the singer and acoustic instruments. The strongest proponent of the p.a. purchase will be the generous, but tired, band member who has been begging, borrowing, hauling, toting and hooking up whatever sound equipment you've used up to this point.

The sound system question is where the rubber meets the road. It is the first of many that will test your commitment to the band enterprise. For one thing, the band members without lives will now want to start practicing at least twice a week. ("If I'm going to get paid for something, I want it to be damn good," they'll say.) Others will just want to keep jamming as informally as possible. ("I thought we were doing this for fun.") If you stay together – a continuing concern – you will have to find a happy medium on such issues. The only given is that you'll **have to** build up your song list. That means acquiring at least 30 to 40 tunes for the ultimate four-hour dance gig. That requires more practice of some sort, particularly since you now will have to work at standard beginnings and endings for each one, which is a major part of making a tune sound polished. More practice, of course, means more commitment on the part of all concerned.

What we're talking about is a set of relationships that have to work if you're going to make music. That's what is hard – and rewarding – about playing in a band. The problems can be as complex as the musicians you meet. Recently, I sat across a restaurant table from two women musicians who without a trace of humor informed me of what they see as the almost insurmountable difficulties created for women players by the boys-club nature of most bands. As best I can understand the situation from my male perspective, the boys-club atmosphere drives many women players away. The buddy-buddy nurturing that men give and get from each other just doesn't get through to many women and/or doesn't work for them. (I suspect this is because they speak a different language than men, which is grist for a another whole book; see *You Just Don't Understand* by Deborah Tanner.) Of course, I am also being kinder to men than my women friends were. I tend to explain this problem in terms of a failure to communicate. My women friends were more inclined to use words like insensitive, clod, selfish, self-centered, egotistical and worse.

No matter how you describe this breach between musicians of opposite sex, it is part of a major dilemma faced by all people who want to start a band and make interesting music. The tendency of groups of musicians to isolate themselves from one another is disturbing, whether the isolated groups be men and women, jazzists and classicists, rockers and cowboys, or whatever. Music can't grow unless people with different ideas and outlooks get together and share what they know. The key to making that happen is figuring out how to nurture and get along with your musical friends.

Money

Our final advice on forming a band is: Please don't even consider doing it for money or the gigs. Do it for the music and the friendships. If music and friends aren't enough and you really do want to play in bars, for weddings and at dances, don't even do that for the money. Do it for the adventure and great stories you'll be able to tell your grandchildren. Money and fame may be in the cards. You might also win the lottery. If these things are going to come, they will. However, if money and fame are not in the cards, you and a realistic attitude will at least end up with joyful memories of music, friends and adventure, which in most cases is preferable to the frustration, bitterness and disillusion of setting your heart on things not likely to happen.

When I wrote this chapter the first time, the biggest concern in our little band wasn't that our first paid gig was a week away, but that

Mike, our rhythm guitarist, might burn himself out working too hard. Several weeks back, he had separated from his wife and business partner. Until then, he had worked 10-hour days, volunteered for whatever needed to be done in the evening, would play music any time or place and always showed up bursting with more energy and confidence than any of the rest of us. He's the one who poured me full of beer so I'd have the nerve to play in public the first time. He's the one who encouraged Ron to start singing.

Then, after his separation, he had begun working 12-hour days, sometimes begged off or called to cancel practice, showed up looking weary, went home early to "get some sleep" and said things like, "Oh, baby, this divorce stuff is harder than I thought it'd be." Watching him, we figured Mike would be all right, but still worried about him. After a year, he wasn't just some guy who played guitar pretty well.

Last Minute Update on the Band

As this book began the final downhill schuss toward printing, Men in Shorts, sad to say, played what has been billed alternatively as its last gig or first reunion. By then, the personnel already had changed a lot. Bob left first to go to graduate school. He was replaced by a series of ever more skillful bass players, most of whom didn't work out for reasons that can't be explained without risking libel. Mike left to move to California for love-related reasons. Some months later, Ron bailed out because our gigs began interfering with his job. Ironically, the band started to fold a few months down the road when our latest and greatest bass player found he needed to play *more* gigs to put bread on the table. The tent came down when Pat, our drummer, decided to move with Ron's replacement in a new musical direction, i.e., starting another band. I'm currently working up a set list with yet another singing, guitar-playing pal.

17

Teaching Yourself

As we've said before, we don't really recommend trying to teach yourself to play music. That's the hard way. Music is an oral tradition, handed down by word of mouth and demonstration from one generation to the next. That will always be the case, no matter how many books, CDs, cassettes, scores and video tapes are produced. Even this book is just a tool to make that oral process more efficient. Some day, virtual reality may come a little closer to replacing human teachers, but even that will still be canned. It won't be able to respond to your unique questions or evaluate your unique needs at any given moment.

You'll Need Assistance

If you insist upon teaching yourself, you must be tough enough to persist and bold enough to ask other people for help because we're not really talking about *literally* teach-

A Note to the True Loner

If you are so stubborn, poor and/or introverted that you must learn strictly from books, tapes and video cassettes without the help of any other humans, then we wish you luck, but don't have a lot more specific advice. Your best bet is to find books, videos, etc. that expand upon the concepts we've prescribed. We could write a book with all that detailed information in it, but don't believe it would be a good use of our time or yours, because that detail is hard to write and harder to read. You can get the same material much more easily from a living, breathing human.

ing yourself, locking yourself in a room with your instrument and working with it all alone until you can play. What we're really talking about is learning with guidance from:

- Musician friends; and
- Books, CDs, tapes and video cassettes.

If you can't or won't hire a teacher, you really need to cultivate musical acquaintances, persuading them to give you free what you otherwise have to buy from a teacher.

If you want to pursue this kind of free guidance without making yourself a complete pain in the rear, you'll first need to acquire a little knowledge on your own. Probably the best place to get that little bit of information is in the first five to ten pages of any beginning book on the instrument you want to play. Such books are a good investment as a reference, in any case, because they provide basic information on fingering, musical notation, scales, chords, etc. You'll also want to tinker with the instrument, figuring out what makes it tick, how to get tones out of it and how to play whatever you can by ear.

As soon as you do that, you're ready to take the first step into our method – learning a blues scale and then using a few notes from it to improvise along with a recorded rhythm section. You can find blues scales in an appendix at the back of this book, but will want to ask somebody to demonstrate how to play simple riffs with them. This may sound like a easy question, but you can get a variety of responses, depending on the kind of person you ask.

College and University Music Professors

A college or university music department is a natural place to look for help. That's where you'll find some of the people with the most knowledge about music. Unfortunately, you probably won't get a bunch of advice out of a music faculty member at a college or university unless you sign up for a course or private lessons first. They're busy people who get paid to spend their time teaching their students about music.

Of course, if you catch someone on a good day or happen to run into a really nice person, you may get a positive response. Hopefully, this nice prof plays jazz, rock, blues, etc. If he or she is strictly a classical musician, he or she probably can show you a blues scale, but most likely won't show you a lot about what to do with it because that's not what classical players do, even if they're college professors.

On the other hand, if the prof is a jazzist, you may run into another kind of problem. He or she may completely ignore your specific request and launch directly into a bunch of complicated talk about how you first ought to learn the major scale, modes, chords, chord changes and how to read music, almost none of which you will understand. Your major task will be to bring this fountain of knowledge back to the original request with something like: "I really appreciate everything you're telling me, but I want to learn by the method outlined in this book and what I'd really like to know right now is how to play a simple riff using two or three notes of a blues scale." If this person is really nice, he

Finding Advice on Technique

While you obviously have to get advice about improvising from people who improvise, you can obtain valuable guidance on technique from anybody who plays your instrument well. Classical players usually approach their instruments differently than jazzers and rockers, but still can give you invaluable information about how to fret a guitar, tongue notes on a saxophone or move along a piano's keyboard.

or she will finally show you what you want, but will in the end most likely send you packing with the recommendation that you sign up for a class or private lessons.

College Music Students

A more likely source of continuing help is college music students who play jazz, rock, blues, country, etc. They, too, know lots about music, but may not be accustomed to getting paid for their advice and usually will have more time to talk with you. Moreover, they tend to not be so set in their ways or so certain of the rightness of their personal biases, probably because they don't have a doctorate confirming the correctness of their biases.

These kids – if they play jazz, rock, etc. – should be fully capable of showing you a blues scale and how to toss off some simple riffs. The danger again is that they will quickly move into information too complex for you to absorb. Your job is to keep them focused and learn what you came to find out. Pick up whatever extra information you can, but avoid overload, at all costs.

The nice thing about these kids is that if you make good use of what they tell you, they'll probably have the free time to sit down with you again. They'll probably want to do it, too. Almost everybody likes it when you take their advice and benefit from it.

Bar Band Musicians of the Rock, Blues and Country Variety

These folks are less likely to give you a lecture on music theory and more likely to quickly show you how to play the blues scale you asked about. When it comes to showing you a riff, however, they're apt to illustrate something lightning fast with a bunch of notes, some fancy picking and two or three bends thrown in just to impress you. In which case, you'll have to bring them back to your original request: "That was really cool, but couldn't you just show me something simple and slow with two or three notes?" If you can get them to focus, they can do that. Like the college students, they're also likely to welcome you back when you return, having mastered the first thing they showed you. If you cultivate them properly, these people can be a great resource for answering future questions. The place they may come up short is down the road when you want to learn about reading music or the theory behind what they do on stage in a bar. A lot of people who play well don't know any of the theoretical stuff. For that, you may want to go back to the college jazz students or faculty.

School Music Teachers, Band Directors, Church Choir Directors, Etc.

These people are likely to want to help, but may not know much about improvisation (unless they also play jazz, rock, blues or country on the side, in which case they fall into a better-educated category of bar band musician). If they don't improvise, the best assistance they'll give at this point is to help you puzzle out a blues scale and how to play it. They're still well worth cultivating, however. They know lots about technique, they know lots of great songs, and they have a wealth of theoretical knowledge that will be useful down the road when you want to know more music theory such as chord structure, scales, harmony, etc.

Hobby Musicians — People Who Play at Home for Fun

These people are all over the board. They'll be most helpful if they're improvisers who play blues, country, rock, jazz, etc. If so, they'll be helpful in the same way as the bar band folks, though perhaps less proficient and/or knowledgeable. The advantage is they'll probably be more excited about sitting around talking or playing music with you for hours on end. If they play by reading, by memory (such as fiddle players who know standard tunes) or by ear, they'll be like the church choir director who can help you puzzle out a blues scale, but won't be much help at showing you licks. Once again, however, they're still invaluable because they know songs, lots about technique and tons of other stuff that you'll want to know as you grow more proficient.

Other Novices

As unlikely as it may sound, the most valuable accomplice of all may be another avid novice, who doesn't know much more than you, but is eager to learn. He or she not only will spend lots of time showing you what he or she knows (and playing it with you), but also will help you track down and learn the other things you want to know. As always, two heads are better than one.

The Bottom Line on Finding Assistance

As you may have discerned, the above discussion leads to several conclusions:

- You can get good general information about your instrument from anybody who plays it.
- At the start, the best help with our improvisation-based method will come from generous bar band musicians and amateurs who play jazz, rock, blues, country, etc.
- Later, you'll want to consult with "educated" musicians when you reach the parts of the method where you need to acquire more music theory.
- Every musician can provide you valuable information and help, but many can also lead you astray. We've pared this learning process down to its essentials. If you can keep yourself on the

path we've mapped, you'll get to your destination – a basic proficiency – more quickly.

Books, Videos, CDs and Cassettes

You'll obviously want to augment whatever human help you find with instructional materials. If you're not sure where to find such things, consult our chapter on "Other Books, CDs, Videos, Etc."

18

OTHER BOOKS, CDS VIDEOS, ETC.

Unfortunately, there is no handy one-stop marketplace for all of the good (and not so good) music instruction materials that have been produced over the years. Since they're not big money-makers for a lot of music stores, you'll often find a modest selection on their shelves. To get a true picture of what is available, you'll need to check several sources:

- *Different Kinds of Music Stores:* Don't just go to one music store. If your hometown has several stores, go to all of them, because they usually try to carve out different niches in the market. In Boise, for example, we have a couple of mainstream music stores that sell almost everything, including a lot of instruction books and sheet music. We have another mainstream store that sells mostly pianos. We have a hip rock 'n' roll store that specializes in guitars, drums and electronics. We have another hip store that also caters to guitarists, but leans more to the acoustic side. We have a mall store that sells mostly electronic keyboards. We have a couple more stores that fall somewhere in between the hip and the mainstream elements. And we have a couple of stores that sell used instruments. You'll find different instructional materials at each one.
- *Big Book Stores*: The new megabookstores like Borders and Barnes

& Noble carry a surprisingly rich selection of music books. Check them out. They sometimes have things you won't find in your neighborhood music store.

- *Jamey Aebersold Jazz, Inc.*: Jamey Aebersold pioneered the jazz play-along and instructional material business 20 years ago and is still its leading guru. Most of his stuff is aimed at intermediate to advanced players, but his mail-order house is a wealth of information for all musicians. You can get his free catalogue by calling (800) 456-1388, by fax at (812) 949-2006 or by mail at P.O. Box 1244C, New Albany, IN 474151-1244.
- *Music For People's Resource Catalogue*: Music For People is a national organization dedicated to helping anybody and everybody learn to play improvised music. You can order its catalogue and get other information by phone at (203) 938-0367, by fax at (203) 938-0329 or by mail at 376 Newtown Turnpike, Redding, CT 06896.
- *Music Books Plus*: This Canadian-based company sells books, audio tapes and videos on subjects ranging from instrumental instruction to getting started in the music business to putting together a demo tape. For a catalogue, call (800) 265-8481, send a fax to (905) 641-1648, post an e-mail to order@nor.com or write to 2315 Whirlpool Ave., #132, Niagara Falls, NY 14305.
- *Homespun Tapes*: Guitarist Happy Traum, founder of Homespun Tapes, sells lots of instructional videos, books, etc.,some of which use approaches similar to ours. Most his materials are for guitars and other plucked instruments, but in his catalogue you'll also find help with keyboards, violin and some folk instruments. The catalogue is available by calling (800) 338-2737, by fax at (914) 246-5282 or by mail at Box 694, Woodstock, NY 12498.
- *Mix Bookshelf*: This is the only other catalogue we know of that is

limited to music-related books, videos, etc. It lists a ton of stuff sold by the mail-order operation run by the publishers of *Mix Magazine* and *Electronic Musician*. It's available free by calling (800) 233-9604, by fax at (510) 653-5142 or by mail at 6400 Hollis St. #10, Emeryville, CA 94608.

- *Other Mail-Order Houses*: A number of big mail-order firms sell instruments, books, equipment, etc. Some of them sell everything musical under the sun. Others specialize in specific kinds of instruments and gear. Almost all their catalogues have a section on instructional materials. You can find their ads in music magazines. Below is a sampling of the music magazines sold on the best newstand in Boise:
    - *Country Guitar.*
    - *Down Beat.*
    - *Jazz Player.*
    - *Guitar Player.*
    - *Windplayer.*
    - *Piano & Keyboard.*
    - *Strings.*
    - *Keyboard.*
    - *Modern Drummer.*
    - *Saxophone Journal.*
    - *Electronic Musician.*

19

Buying an Instrument (And Assorted Toys)

Though this may sound obvious, the first decision you have to make when buying an instrument is what "kind" of instrument to buy. Presumably, you know you want to play electric guitar, not sax, but what kind of electric guitar do you want to play? Do you want to sound like Chet Atkins or Keith Richards? If you want to play country like Chet, you might want a Gibson Country Gentleman. If you're an old-fashioned rocker like Keith, you'd probably love a Fender Stratocaster.

If you're looking to play sax, do you want to play soprano like Kenny G, alto like Charlie Parker or tenor like Dexter Gordon?

Would-be keyboard players must decide whether they want to play an electronic keyboard / synthesizer, which is portable and has a thousand computerized sounds; an electric piano with a weighted action, which is still portable, but sounds and feels more like a real piano; or that real piano itself, which has a richness of tone and subtlety of touch that is yet to be matched by electronic imitations. (See the discussion of kinds of keyboards in the section on playing the piano.)

Whatever you decide, make your decision based on the sound **you** like and want, not what your teacher or the sales person at the music store likes. Spend some time thinking back over the years to whatever music has led you to want to play. Dig out the records, tapes and CDs that turned you on to the guitar, sax, fiddle or keyboard instruments.

Identify the sound that touches **your** heart or grabs **your** innards.

Once you get a grip on that sound, **then** talk to your teacher, other musicians and sales people about the particular instrument you need to get that sound. Get them to listen to that favorite recording and help you figure out exactly what kind of guitar, sax, fiddle or keyboard your hero or heroine played. That's the kind of instrument you want to buy.

Cost vs. Quality

As a novice buying a musical instrument, you immediately face a dilemma. You hesitate to spend a lot of money because you don't know how serious you are about this enterprise. Yet, you need a good instrument, because a good instrument is lots easier and more fun to play than a cheap one. The good instrument not only "feels" better and works better, it sounds better because its pitch is more accurate and its tone quality prettier. The difference between a cheap instrument and a good one is roughly the same as the difference between a dull knife and a sharp one. You can work with a dull knife, but why would you if you had a choice?

Rental Instruments

Music stores long have tried to ease would-be musicians through this cost dilemma with rent-to-buy programs. This is a pretty good deal. The student gets to try playing, but takes little risk. You can quit any time without suffering a major loss. If you decide to buy, you usually can apply your rental payments to the purchase price of the rented instrument or a new one. The major downside is that rental instruments seldom are great ones. Also, you might be able to find a better deal on a used instrument by looking in pawn shops or the classified ads. On the other hand, if you find a used instrument in a pawn shop or the classifieds, you give up your chance to quickly start a personal relationship with your local music retailer, who can be an invaluable source of information and technical support. Life is full of tough choices.

If you do choose to rent, do it primarily to get a taste of the instrument. As you play the rental, keep in mind that you're working with a handicap – the dull knife we mentioned earlier. Once you can see you're going to stick with this new endeavor, move as quickly as possible into the best instrument you can afford.

New Instruments

As we said above, most music stores will also let you apply rental payments to purchase a new instrument. That's a good deal if you have the money to buy a top-notch new instrument right out of the gate.

Instruments come in three basic qualities:

- Professional instruments, which is what you want;
- Good student instruments, which is what you may have to settle for if funds are limited. Many of these instrument really are good, meaning they work well mechanically and have accurate intonation. There's no reason a student shouldn't buy one – unless you can buy a used professional instrument for the same price, a possibility discussed below; and
- Inexpensive student instruments, some of which are good, others of which should be avoided if possible.

Some companies separate different quality instruments into different product lines. Selmer, which makes some of the world's best horns, sells the best ones under the Selmer label; it sells pretty good instruments under the Signet label; and less expensive ones under the Bundy label. Yamaha, the world's leading instrument maker, sells everything as different models under its own name; the higher the model number – and price – the better the quality.

In either case, buying a new instrument is fairly straightforward. Talk to dealers and musicians to find out the best makers of the type of instrument you want. You'll hear names like Steinway, Baldwin, Yamaha and Kawai for pianos; Selmer, Buffet and Yamaha for saxophones; Selmer, Buffet and Yamaha for clarinets; Fender, Yamaha and Gibson for electric guitars, etc. You won't go too far wrong if you pick one of the best manufacturers and buy the most expensive instrument you can afford.

Like all rules, this one has exceptions, of course. Some Fender Stratocaster guitars cost more than others because of features that don't enhance their basic, high level of playability. Other instruments cost more because of special construction or materials needed to obtain a special sound. A Gibson hollow-body guitar, for example, is no more playable than a Stratocaster, but costs more because of its mellow-sounding hollow-body construction. Similarly, an $8,000 Baldwin baby grand piano might look and sound wonderful in your living room, but is no more playable than a $2,000 Baldwin upright.

Once you research the quality issue and know what you want, the only real trick is negotiating the price you pay. Musical instruments are like cars. You don't necessarily have to pay sticker price. The best way to figure out what you ought to pay your local dealer is to find out the price at one of the big mail-order houses that carry all brands of instruments. That's a rock bottom most local dealers won't hit, but may approach. As with any purchase, you pay a little extra for having someone down the street who'll stand behind the product.

Used Instruments

If you're cost-conscious, you'll want to seriously consider a good used instrument. A well-maintained used instrument is almost always a better deal than a similarly priced new one. In fact, excellent old instruments in many cases cost less than mediocre new ones. They may not look as good, but they work and sound great. Many professional sax players prefer the Selmer Mark VI, which the company quit making 25 years ago. Some pianists have a similar bias. I have an acquaintance who searched several years for a used Steinway grand with just the warm tone quality he sought. He finally found his dream piano in the corner of a recreation room at a nursing home.

Here's the best part of the buying used instruments: Good ones don't go down in value. In fact, most of the really good ones actually go up in value. If you're a savvy shopper, you'll be dollars ahead to buy a good used instrument right from the start of your musical career. If you quit after a few weeks, you can always sell the darn thing at little or no loss. I sold my first tenor sax for exactly what I had paid two years earlier. I bought a better horn for $100 more.

Buying a good used instrument is like buying anything else used. It requires research. Assistance from a neutral third party, like a teacher or working musician, is also helpful. First, you have to identify the good manufacturers and models you would consider buying. Then, when you find what you think is a good buy, you have to be able to tell if it is in good working order. A once-fine piano, for example, is worthless if the pins that secure the strings are too loose and prevent the instrument from being tuned. You're money ahead to pay a good repair person to look over any instrument you hope to buy. He or she can advise whether it can be put back into perfect working order.

And, remember, it doesn't matter how an instrument looks, only how it plays.

Where to Look

The all-time most likely place to find a good deal on a great instrument is the bulletin board of the music department at a college or university. That's where you have the greatest chance of running into a desperately poor player who needs cash right now and is prepared to sacrifice his or her axe at below-market price. The classified ads are another good source of deals. Here, too, you may run into somebody who needs quick money and doesn't know or care about the market price for the instrument.

If you're careful, you also can scare up deals in pawn shops. Be wary, though. It's the rare pawn dealer who doesn't know the exact values of all makes and models of saxes, guitars, trumpets and whatever. Musical instruments are standard fare in the hock shop trade; most dealers have books that tell the going rate for almost every make and model. You stand your best chance of getting a deal when an instrument has been sitting in the shop too long. In that situation, a dealer will drop the price just to move the item, recoup the investment and put that money to work somewhere else. Whatever you do, don't pay the price marked on the tag. That's just a place to start haggling.

The quickest route to a good instrument at market price is a dealer who specializes in high-quality used instruments, either as a major sideline to new sales or as the sole business. You won't find fire-sale rates in this venue, but the quality service and knowledgeable advice in most cases will make up for that inconvenience. Selling used musical instruments is not something people do to get rich. In most cases, they do it because they love not only music, but musical instruments and all the tradition, craftsmanship and lore that go with them. They know, and will generally share, more about instruments than you'll get from most musicians, who may know a few models well, but lack the knowledgeable dealer's broad experience.

Last, but not least, are mainstream music stores that sell some used instruments, but don't really look on them as a primary source of revenue. In most cases, they focus on student model instruments because that's where the cash-flow comes from – the parents of junior high and high school kids.

Other Musical Toys

If you're a gear hog with the money to support your vice, music is the avocation for you. As you learn to play and begin frequenting music stores, you soon will find yourself wondering whether it might be fun and/or useful to acquire some of the exotic gadgets on display. If you have extra money and are at all inclined to be an equipment freak, you'll find plenty of ways to indulge yourself. Below is a listing of what we think are your most sensible options.

Metronomes

A metronome – a device that beats out a steady tempo for you to play along with – is not an option. It's a necessity. Some people have natural rhythm, but most of us learn rhythm and groove by playing along with a steady beat. Most metronomes today are electronic instruments about the size of a pack of cigarettes. We recommend you get one with an earphone, which makes the beat easier to hear when you play loudly. You also can run a cord from the metronome's earphone jack to your stereo amplifier, which is better yet.

Drum Machines

A drum machine is an enticing alternative to a metronome. This little specialty computer not only keeps the basic beat, but also comes with lots of pre-programmed rhythms that can make your practice session more fun. You can run it through your stereo amplifier, too. Most duplicate a variety of percussion instruments, from cymbals and snares to congas and guiros. Once you become adept at operating the machine, you can create your own rhythms and even program drum tracks for entire songs. If you already own a computer, look into drum machine software.

Tape Decks and Microphones

One of the best ways to improve your playing is to record and listen to your practice session. You'll hear a lot that you don't hear while playing. You can do this with the built-in mikes on your ghetto blaster, which works surprisingly well. If you want a better quality sound, you may want to buy a good microphone to plug into your tape deck. (Don't worry if your deck doesn't have a microphone jack. With an adaptor, you can run the mike through the input jacks in the back of the deck.)

An added bonus that comes with ownership of a good microphone is the joy of singing through it. At my house, we run the mike through the stereo amplifier. When my father-in-law, Ed, plays the piano after dinner, we sometimes pass the mike around so everybody gets the chance to sing a solo. It's corny, but fun. You'll be surprised how much better you sing through a good mike.

Multi-Track Tape Recorders

If you really want to have fun with recordings, you may want a multi-track recorder in your future. They're great for playing along with yourself. The least expensive ones have four tracks, which means that you can record on one track, then go back and listen to it on the headphones while you play along with it, recording on a second track, then a third and fourth.

This means you can lay down half a duet, then come back and play the second part along with yourself. If you like harmony, you're guaranteed to have fun with recordings of yourself playing it this way. When you get better, you can create four-part harmony all by your lonesome, which can be just a little bit thrilling.

Of course, when you form a band, you'll want to record it, too. That's when a multi-track becomes a must. The only way to achieve the proper balance of instruments on a recording is to record different instruments on different tracks with separate volume controls for each track. That way, you can adjust the balance after the recording is on tape. For a few hundred bucks, you can buy a recorder that in the hands of a good engineer will make amazingly good tapes. All you have to do is become a good engineer – another fun goal for the equipment-minded.

Rhythm Instruments

As soon as you start making music with other people, you'll probably want to buy some rhythm instruments. They include everything from tambourines to claves, which is just two fat sticks you smack together in time, to maracas, guiros, triangles, cowbells and any number of small drums. With a few of these items in your toy box, any friend can add a musical element to your jam session. Most rhythm instruments cost less than $30 dollars and will provide you more fun per buck than any other musical purchase.

P.A. (Public Address) Systems

When you start playing music with other people, sooner or later you'll need a p.a. system. We've all seen parts of them at concerts – the huge control console with a zillion knobs and wires running off to God knows where. It looks complicated, but the concept is simple.

A p.a. is what the vocalist and some instrumentalists sing and play through for amplification. They sing or play through mikes that run to an amplifier / mixing board, which is more or less an electronic funnel.

Each mike runs first through its own volume controls on the mixing board. These controls let you balance the levels of the instruments and voices. The separate channels then run into the neck of the funnel, mix with the other signals and pass through a master volume control. Finally, the product is output through the speakers.

Most p.a.'s also can enhance the original signal by adding "effects" or boosting the bass, mid-range or treble parts of the signal. You can, for example, turn a skinny little voice like mine into something unrecognizably rich and powerful. This can be fun.

Tuners

An electronic tuner is one tool that every string and horn player should have. They're all but essential for novices, since it takes a while to learn to tune strings or a horn by ear. Needless to say, it's a lot harder to play an instrument that's out of tune. A tuner solves the problem by listening to you play the required pitch and telling you – with a meter needle or LED readout – whether you are sharp, flat or right on. The tuner not only gets you playing in tune faster, it helps you train your ears, too, by letting them know when they're hearing the right pitch. One word of caution. Some players rely so heavily on the tuner that they never develop their ears. Don't do that. After you've been playing a while, start tuning by ear and using the tuner to check your accuracy. Eventually, you won't need the tuner under most circumstances.

Electric Guitar Gizmos

We could write a whole book about the hundreds of devices designed to lure money out of the pockets of electric guitar players, but won't. The one gizmo we recommend for novices is an electronic tuner. Most other devices for electric guitars pump some kind of "effects" like distortion or wah wah into the signal created by the guitar. As you go about developing your sound, you'll want to try out these tools, which can help you discover the exact feel you want to create.

Synthesizers

A synthesizer is a computer that produces and / or reproduces sounds digitally. It consists of a controller such as a keyboard and a brain, which outputs through an amplifier and speakers.

Some synthesizers are instruments used to actually create electronic sounds from scratch. More familiar nowadays are synthesizers that use "sampled" sounds recorded on a disk or microchip. A sampler literally listens to a sample of a sound created acoustically, say by a violin, and records it in the computer brain. Then the brain can use that sample to reproduce clones of the violin sound and put the clones together into musical compositions.

With some synthesizers, you can do the sampling yourself. Most synthesizer owners either use the sampled sounds built into their instrument or on discs purchased separately. The options available include almost all musical instruments and just about any other sound that any wild and crazy person might want to reproduce – freight trains, screams, you name it.

Synthesizer controllers come in all shapes and sizes. The most common are keyboards. Others are played like guitars, violins and even saxophones, which means that if you know how to play guitar, violin or sax, you can play a synthesizer to create any kind of sound you like. It also means that a keyboard can produce what sounds like a whole band by laying down tracks for each instrument, one at a time. Sadly, that's how the entertainment and advertising industries create a lot of commercial music these days, which means they don't hire as many musicians as they once did.

Sequencers

If you get into synthesizers, you no doubt will get into sequencers, too. A sequencer is a device for recording the digital signals created by an electronic keyboard or other controller designed for use with a synthesizer. Basically, the sequencer is a computer memory and the hardware and software to run it. You create a musical composition with your controller in much the same way as you type a letter on your computer. The sequencer records the composition on disc or in a chip, the same way your computer records your letter on disc or in a chip. Finally, the sequencer "outputs" your musical composition through a synthesizer and sound system the same way your computer prints your letter on a printer.

The neat thing about sequencers is that they have multiple channels, so you can lay down tracks with the sounds of different instruments and / or musical parts. That's how one musician with a keyboard makes a recording that sounds like an entire band.

20

SCHOOL BAND AND ORCHESTRA

We've made some pretty strong statements in this book about good and bad methods of teaching music. Please don't think that means we want to toss out the traditional methods used by school bands and orchestras, where so many people learn so much about music. We're not perfectly happy with school music programs, but we're not proposing that they adopt our approach, either, because our approach isn't designed for use with large groups of rowdy students in a classroom setting.

Our biggest complaint about school music programs is that most students who go through them quit making music after high school. Band and orchestra students acquire an incredible amount of knowledge about music and technique on their instruments. Yet, after they leave school, all that knowledge and hard-won skill go to waste. More than 90 percent put their horn or violin away, never to play again.

We believe the main reason these young graduates forsake their instruments is that they never learned to play the improvised music that is most popular in our culture or to play in small groups, which is the easiest, most relaxed way to have fun with music.

Our Suggestions

If we could, we would reinvent school music curricula to assure that music students learn to improvise and play in small groups, but we're not sure we have the expertise to take on that rather awesome task. Instead, we would like to make several of suggestions to music educators:

Set the Goal of Creating Lifetime Musicians: The first suggestion is that music educators make it their goal that every one of their students will become a lifetime musician, playing some kind of music for pleasure the rest of his or her days. Simply setting a goal often initiates the innovating thinking that makes things happen.

Promote Improvising as an Extracurricular Activity: The second suggestion is that educators encourage junior high and high school music students to follow our approach to improvised music **in addition** to what they learn in the band and orchestra room. It isn't hard to quickly introduce young players to the concept of improvising over 12-bar blues and how to pursue the concept on their own with small groups of friends. It can be done in a few workshops. Bob conducted such workshops when he was student-teaching in Texas, and we've done it together at high schools here in Boise. A few schools around the country do it all the time. A taste of improvising is all that most serious band and orchestra students need to get them going, because the prospect of really playing the blues is so exciting that they quickly turn a little bit of knowledge into a major compulsion. Once someone shows them how the 12-bar blues form works and illustrates how to improvise using a blues scale, eager students will take off on their own and start figuring out the rest by themselves. The real secret is in keeping the workshops simple. Diving too quickly into more complex chord changes, jazz theory, modes and the like can kill the enthusiasm of a would-be improviser more quickly than anything, simply by making this pastime look more complicated than it really is.

Get Horn and String Players Together with Guitarists and Pianists: The third suggestion is that educators do whatever it takes to get band and orchestra students together in small groups with young guitar players, bassists and drummers who are learning to improvise on their own, because that's the way those instruments usually are learned. Have them drag in piano students taking private lessons, too. A lot of garage band kids can open the door to improvising for horn, string and piano students in a single sitting. Once that happens, the band, orchestra and piano players can teach the garage banders a lot about music and technique. Putting all these kids together, combining their formal and informal training, is like mixing the chemical components of gunpowder. The result is an explosion of musical innovation.

Promote Playing in Small Groups: If we had our way, every band and orchestra student in the country would have to take a seminar on how to organize and play with a small ensemble, whether a string quartet playing Mozart or a blues band. It just makes sense if you want people to keep playing after high school. Few adults are ever going to play in community bands or orchestras. Many, however, would play in small groups with friends if they got a taste of that desirable pastime while still in school. It's just an easier, more relaxed and fun kind of thing to do.

Provide Every Student the Opportunity to Take Private Lessons: Finally, we all know that if music students are going to become truly proficient, which makes them much more likely to continue playing after high school, most need to take private lessons at some point. Schools don't have to leave that opportunity to chance just because some kids don't have the money to pay for individual instruction. When Bob was student-teaching in Texas, he worked in high schools where the band boosters made sure every student got the chance to take private lessons if he or she wanted to take them. In the best programs, private teachers actually worked in practice rooms on the high school campus through an arrangement with the school district, which made it a lot easier for kids to get to lessons. For kids who lacked the money to pay, the boosters provided scholarships supported by their fund-raising activities.

21

GLOSSARY

Articulation: The way a musician starts or "attacks" a note. It can range from a smooth slurring slide into the note to a machine-gun blat to a quiet tick tick tick.

Ballad: For our purposes, a slow, expressive tune.

Bar: Technically, a bar is the vertical line that separates measures on the staff in musical notation. However, in common usage, the word bar has become interchangeable with the word measure. So, for our purposes, a bar or measure in a song is a unit of the passage of time, which has a specific number of beats, depending on the time signature of the song. All of the music discussed in this book has four beats to the measure, which is the case for most blues, rock, country and other popular music.

Barre Chord: A technique for playing chords on a guitar or other fretted instrument in which the index finger acts as a "bar" holding down all the strings at a specified fret, while other fingers fret specific notes further up the neck.

Blues Scale: The six-note scale often used to improvise over straight blues such as those played by electric blues bands. It is made up of the root, minor third, fourth, flatted fifth, fifth, and lowered seventh tones.

C Blues Scale

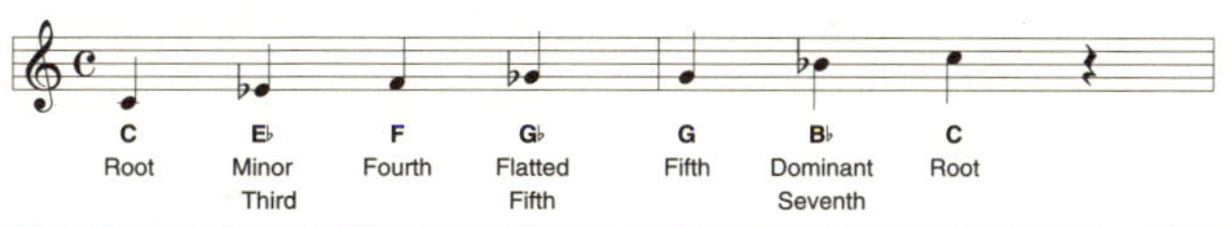

Chops: A musician's technical ability at the moment, as in "How are your chops?" Chops go up or down depending how much the musician has been playing and practicing. In a narrower sense, the term refers to the condition of a horn player's embouchure, i.e., the connection between his or her mouth and the mouthpiece.

Chord: For our purposes, two or more notes played together to create a particular sound or emotion. (Technically, a two-note "chord" is really called an interval.)

Chord Progression: A series of chords played in a specific order with a specific duration for each chord to create the skeleton of a song. If two songs have the same chord progression, they may have different rhythms, tempos, dynamics and words, but are still essentially the same.

Chromatic Scale: The musical scale made up of half-steps. It is played by moving from one key to the next on a piano (including the black keys) or from one fret to the next on a guitar.

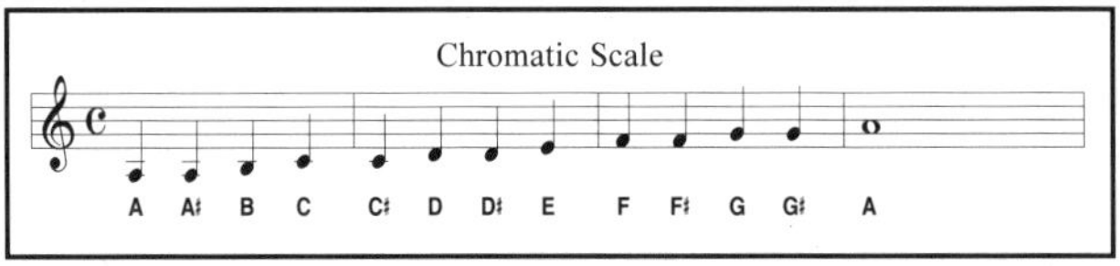

Comp: To play rhythm in the background while another musician solos or sings, i.e., to play the chord progression of a tune in a specified rhythm. The term usually is applied to the piano, guitar or other instrument that plays chords.

Dorian Scale: This is a minor-sounding scale played by starting on the second note of a major scale and playing up or down until you get to that note again. For example, a D dorian scale is just the C major scale played from D to D. (If you think of the major scale as do re mi fa so la ti do, then the related Dorian scale would be re mi fa so la ti do re.) This scale is a good one for soloing over minor blues tunes.

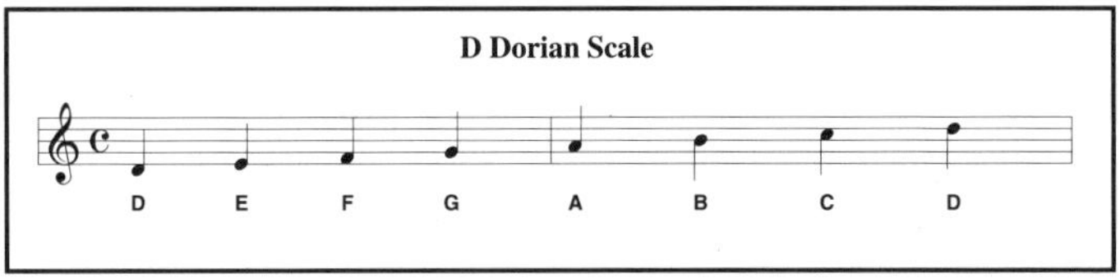

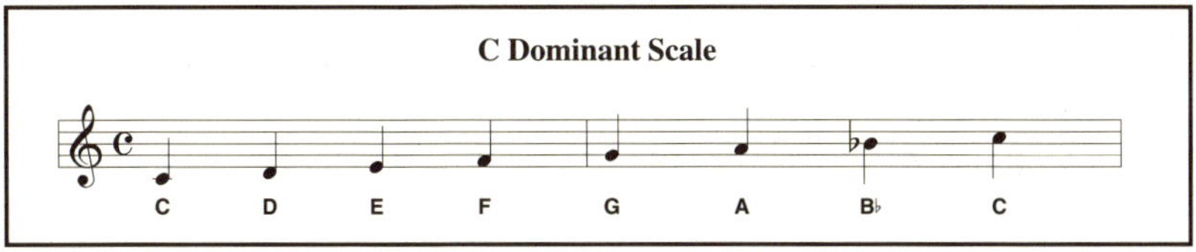

Dominant Scale: This scale is the same as a major scale, except that the major seventh is lowered a half step.

Dominant Seventh Chord: The chord made up of the root, the major third, the fifth and the lowered seventh.

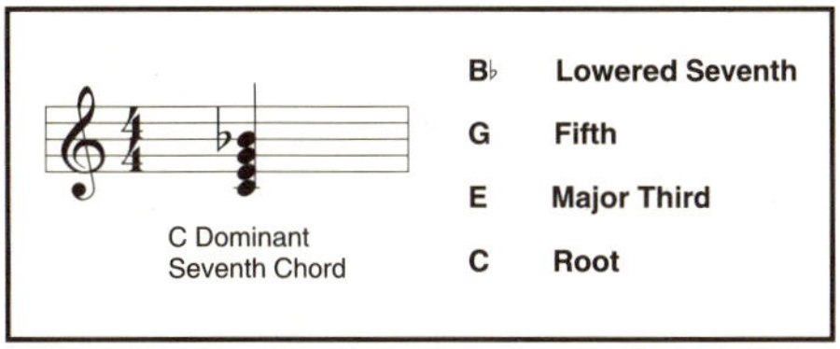

Dominant Seventh: For our purposes, a lowered major seventh, i.e., the note a half step below a major seventh or a full step below the root. (Technically, calling this note a dominant seventh probably is not quite right, but a lot of players do, so you can, too.)

Dynamics: The change in volume in various parts of a piece of music to create different moods.

Embouchure: The way a horn player applies his or her lips to the mouthpiece of a wind instrument.

Fingering Chart: A chart that shows how to finger each note on a musical instrument.

Fifth: For our purposes, the fifth note of a major scale. (Technically, the term fifth describes an interval along the major scale. It is seven half steps, which is the distance between the root of the major scale and the fifth note in the scale.)

Flat: When used as an adjective to describe a note (e.g., that note was "flat"), flat means the note being played was lower in pitch than it should have been. As a noun (e.g. B-flat), the flat is the note a half tone lower than the note it modifies. The symbol for flat is ♭.

Fourth: For our purposes, the fourth note of a major scale. (Technically, the term fourth describes an interval along the major scale. It is five half steps, which is the distance between the root of the major scale and the fourth note in the scale.)

Fret: Frets are the metal ridges across the neck of a guitar, banjo, etc. By pressing a string against a fret, you shorten its length and raise the pitch of the tone.

Grace Note: An "extra" note played quickly to lead into a melody note. In piano blues, it is used to obtain a bluesy effect similar to that of "bending" a note on guitar or sax. The pianist does this by striking a grace note a half step above or below the melody note, then quickly sliding to the melody note.

Half Step: The basic unit of musical distance in Western (as opposed to Oriental) music. There are 12 half steps as is illustrated below.

Interval: The musical distance between two notes, for example, a fifth, major third, minor third, etc.

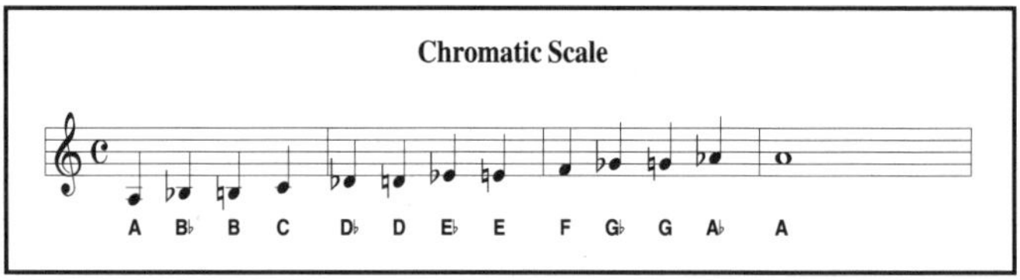

Inversion: A way of playing a chord to get a different sound by "inverting" the notes of the chord. For example, the root position of a C major chords is C - E - G, with the E higher than the C and the G higher than the E. An inversion would be to play G - C - E, using the G that falls below the C and E.

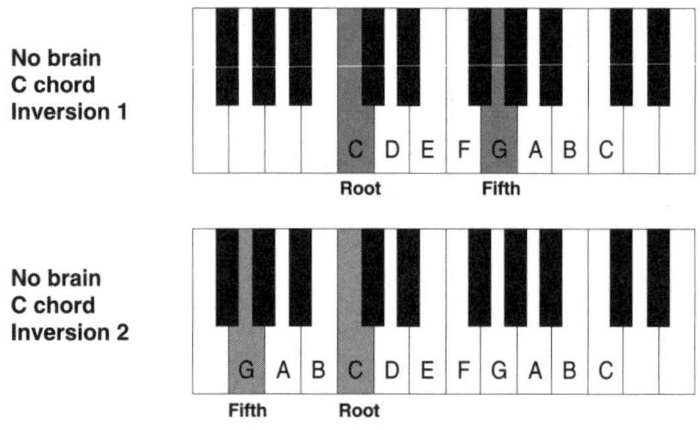

Inversion

An inversion of a chord is just a different combination of the chord tones, as shown in the illustration above. In each case, the chord is the same, but each inversion will sound different.

Key Signature: The sharps or flats on the beginning of a staff of music, which identify the notes that are sharp or flat and, thus, define the key of the song.

Key Signature

A key signature is a group of sharps or flats on the staff, usually at the beginning of a tune. It tells you which notes are lowered or raised a half tone. It also tells you the key of the tune. Don't try to puzzle out how it tells you the key right not. It's not worth the effort at this point.

Lick: A short musical statement. It could be made up of as few as two or three notes or could be several measures long and run through a lot of notes. Also called a riff.

Linear Soloing: Creating a solo by selecting notes from a scale that works with the key of the tune. Linear simply means "in a line." That's how you use the notes from the scale, stringing them together, one after another. Also called "horizontal" soloing, as opposed to "vertical" soloing, which is defined elsewhere in the glossary.

Major Blues: A jazzy blues sound that can be obtained by soloing using the notes of the blues scale from the related minor key of the key in which the tune is being played. (For example, if the tune is played in C, then the related minor key is A. If the tune is played in G, then the related minor key is E.) Some people get what we call a major blues sound by soloing using the notes of the major pentatonic scale of the key in which the tune is played. Like jazz players, country music people also use this sound a lot.

Major Chord (or Major Triad): The chord made up of the root, major third and fifth.

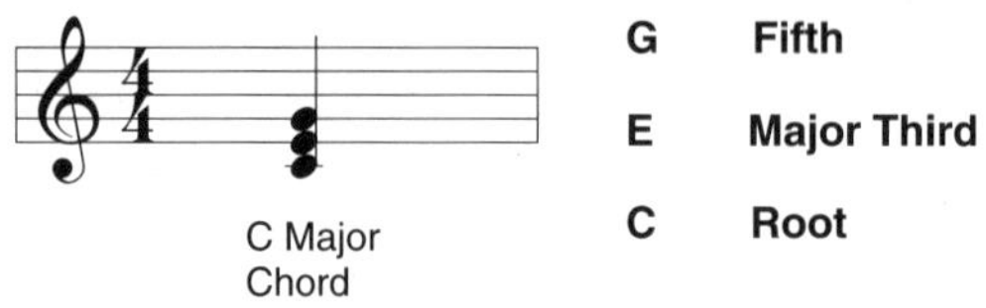

Major Pentatonic Scale: The scale made up of the root, second, third, fifth and sixth of a major scale.

C Major Pentatonic Scale

Major Scale: The seven-note-to-an-octave scale that most of us think of when we think of a scale, i.e., do re mi fa so la ti do.

C Major Scale

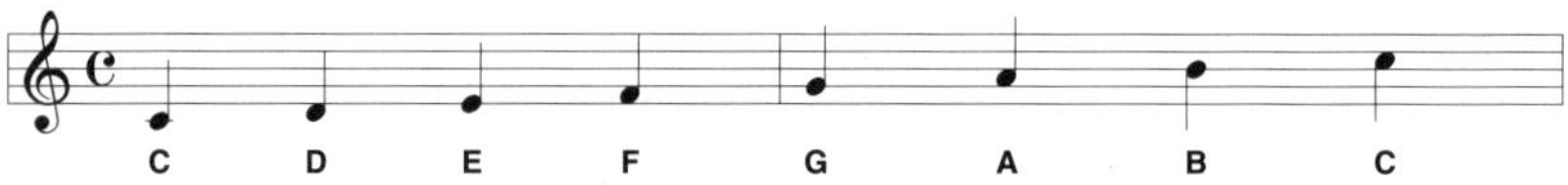

Major Third: For our purposes, the major third is the third note of a major scale. (Technically, the term major third describes an interval along the major scale. It is four half steps, which is the distance between the root of the major scale and the third note in the scale, i.e., the major third.)

Major Seventh: For our purposes, the major seventh is the seventh note of a major scale. (Technically, the term major seventh describes an interval along the

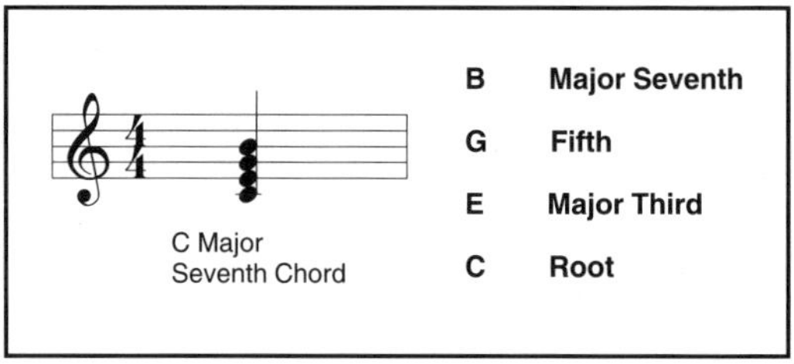

major scale. It is 11 half steps, which is the distance up the scale from the root of the major scale to the seventh note in the scale.)

Major Seventh Chord: The chord made up of the root, major third, fifth and seventh.

Measure: A unit of the passage of time in music that is made up of a specific number of beats. All the music discussed in this book has four beats to the bar or measure. In common usage, a measure is often called a bar, although technically that's not quite right. (See the definition of "bar" for an explanation.)

Melody: The "tune" that we usually associate with a specific song. It is actually just a series of notes, each of which sounds good with the chord being played. The melody by which you identify a song is just one of many that will work with the song's chord progression.

Minor Chord (or Minor Triad): The chord made up of the root, minor third and fifth.

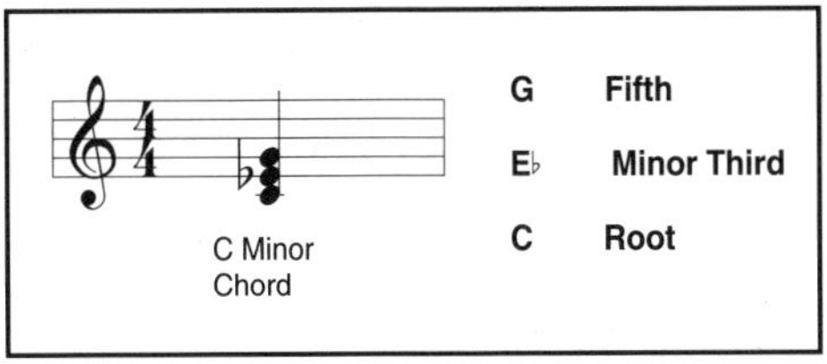

Minor Third: The minor third is the note a half step below the major third. The term minor third also is used to describe an interval along the major scale. It is three half steps, i.e, the distance from the root of the scale to the minor third.

Minor Seventh Chord: The chord made up of the root, minor third, fifth and lowered seventh.

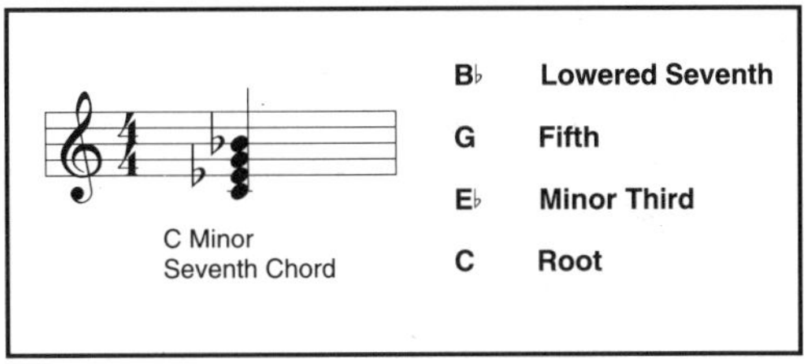

Music Theory: The study of how music and its various elements work.

Octave: The distance on the scale from one A to another A, one B to another B, etc. A note that is an octave above another has exactly twice as many vibrations per second as the lower.

I chord, II chord, III chord, etc.: These terms refer to chords in whatever key you're talking about. The roman numeral indicates the note of the major scale that is the root of the chord. For example, if you're talking about the key of C, then the I chord in the key of C is the chord based on the first note of the C major scale, i.e., C. The II chord is the chord based on the second note of the major scale, i.e., D. And so on and so forth.

Open Chord: A technique for playing chords on a guitar or other fretted instrument, in which some of the strings are played "open" or unfretted, while others are fretted.

Pitch: What most people think of as the "highness" or "lowness" of a tone.Technically, the quality of a tone determined by the frequency of the vibration of the sound wave reaching the ear (the greater the frequency, the higher the pitch);

Procrastinate: To put something off until another day. (Don't do this with music!)

Related Minor: The related minor key is the minor key that has the same key signature as its related major, i.e., that has the same notes at the related major, but sounds different (minor) because you start the scale at a different place. The related minor starts a minor third below the original key. (For example, the related minor of C is A; for G, it's E; for B, it's G#, etc.)

Riff: A short musical statement. It could be made up of as few as two or three notes or could be several measures long and run through a lot of notes. Also called a lick.

Root Note: The note upon which a chord is based, e.g., A for the A major chord, C for the C major chord, etc.

Rhythm Section: The part of a band that provides the foundation of a song by playing both the rhythm and the chord progression of the song while other members perform solos or sing. The most common rhythm section is made up of a drummer, bassist and pianist or rhythm guitarist.

Scale: A series of notes that are a prescribed musical distance apart. The most familiar is the major scale: do re mi fa so la ti do, but there are lots of different scales for different kinds of music.

Scale Patterns: Exercises made up of (What else?) patterns of notes from a scale. If you call the notes of a scale 1,2,3,4,5 and 6, then a scale pattern might look like 1 2 3 4, 2 3 4 5, 3 4 5 6, 4 5 6 1, etc. Once you get into playing an instrument, practicing scale patterns can help you develop your ability to get around on the instrument.

Sharp: When used as an adjective to describe a note (e.g., that note was "sharp"), the term sharp means the note being played is higher in pitch than it should be. As a noun (e.g. C-sharp), the sharp is the note a half tone higher than the note it modifies. The symbol for a sharp is ♯.

Solo Transcription: An improvised solo that has been written down in musical notation. Doing this involves long hours of sitting by a record player, CD player or tape deck, listening to each phrase of a tune over and over again until you figure out the notes and can write them down. Lots of famous solos have been transcribed and can be purchased at music stores.

Staff: In musical notation, the system of five lines and four spaces upon which notes are written.

Technique: The way a player manipulates his or her instrument to move from note to note.

Tablature: A special kind of musical notation for stringed instruments, which shows how the notes are fretted.

Guitar Tablature

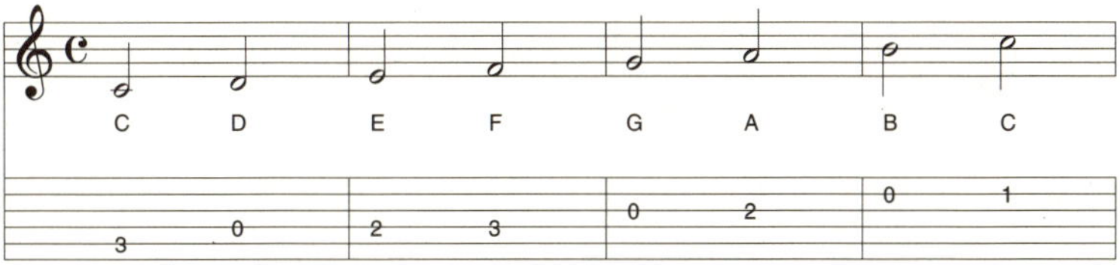

In guitar tablature, as shown above, the lower "staff" represents the strings of a guitar. The lowest string is the low E, then the A, the D, the G, the B and the high E. A number on the string indicates the fret you must hold down to play the note shown in musical notation above the

Tempo: The speed or velocity of a tune, usually expressed in beats per minute.

Time Signature: The symbol at the beginning of a song that looks like a fraction (4/4, 2/4, 6/8, etc.) The top number tells you the number of beats in a measure. The bottom number tells you the type of note that represents one beat. A 4 tells you it's a quarter note, an 8 indicates an eighth note, etc.

Trading Fours: Two players are said to be trading fours when they alternate their playing, each soloing for four bars, then resting while the other solos for four bars.

Transpose: To translate a piece of music from one key to another, note by note.

12-bar blues: 12-bar blues is the most common blues form, the standard, so to speak. It has a standard length of 12 bars or measures of four beats each. It also has a standard chord progression. There are many variations of the standard chord progression, but those don't matter to a novice. At the start, you can play any 12-bar blues tune as though it has the following progression.

Easiest Basic Blues

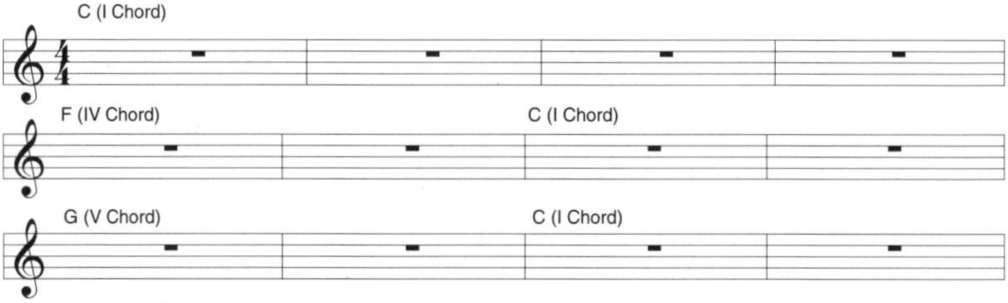

Literally hundreds of well-known rock, country and blues songs are 12-bar blues, which makes them all basically the same except for their rhythm and words.

Vertical Soloing: Creating a solo that focuses primarily on the tones of the chord being played at any given time. The "vertical" name comes from the fact that in musical notation the notes of a chord are usually stacked one upon another as shown in the diagram. Contrast this with the concept of "horizontal or linear" soloing, which is defined elsewhere. Not all musicians use these terms, but we find they help students understand different ways to get different sounds.

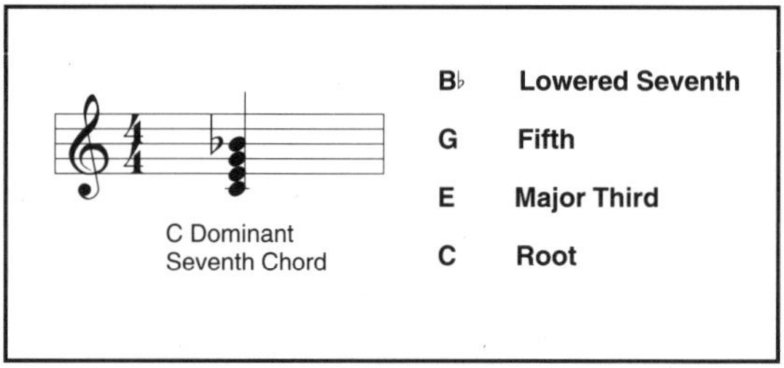

Vibrato: A large part of the warmth that most musicians seek in their sound comes from this hard-to-define effect, which at its most obvious is the sound a player makes when he or she holds a long tone and makes it quaver with a golden wahwahwah- wahwahwahwah.

Whole Step: In Western (as opposed to Oriental) music, a whole step is the musical distance made up of two half steps, e.g., the distance from A to B. (It's a half step from A to B♭ and another half step from B♭ to B.)

1 APPENDIX

Basic Shuffle Rhythm Pattern

The music below shows the basic shuffle rhythm discussed in Chapter 8. If you don't read music well enough to understand it, any decent guitarist or piano player can look at this and show you how it sounds. The part that gives it the shuffle feel is the pairing of each dotted eight and sixteenth note to give a tah ta, tah ta, tah ta rhythm.

(For an explanation of guitar tablature, see the glossary.)

Basic Shuffle Rhythm Pattern

12-Bar Blues in A

APPENDIX

Alternative Form of the Basic Shuffle Rhythm Pattern

The music below shows the alternative, Jimmy-Reed-style version of the shuffle rhythm discussed in Chapter 8. Again, if you can't figure out how it sounds by reading the music, any decent guitarist or piano player can look at this and show you how it sounds.

Alternative Form of Basic Shuffle Rhythm Pattern

3

APPENDIX

Basic Rock Rhythm Pattern

The music below shows the basic, Chuck-Berry-style rock rhythm discussed in Chapter 8. What gives it the rock feel is the pairing of eighth notes to create a ta ta, ta ta, ta ta, ta ta rhythm.

Again, any decent guitarist or piano player can look at this and show you how it's played.

Basic Rock Rhythm Pattern

12-Bar Blues in A, Chuck Berry Style

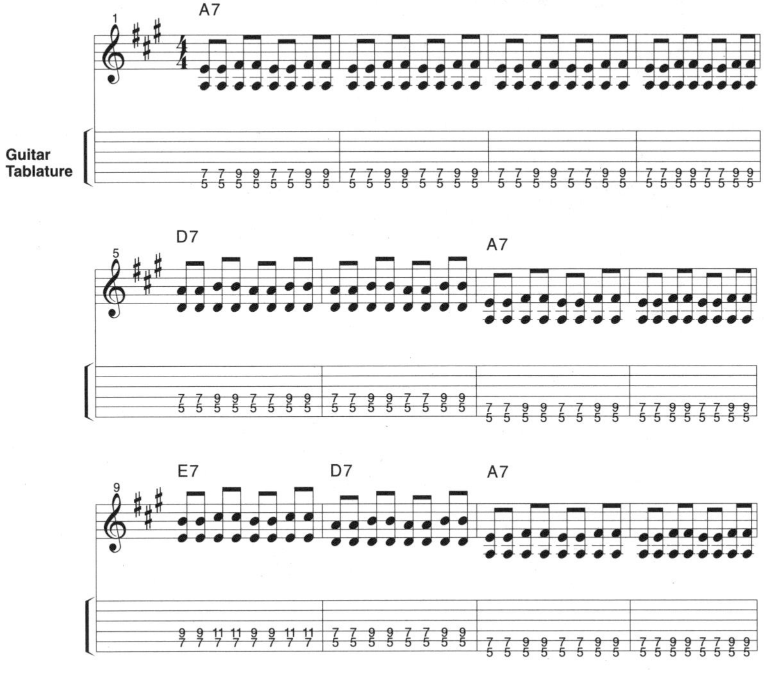

4

APPENDIX

Alternative Form of the Basic Rock Rhythm Pattern

The music below shows the alternative form of the basic rock rhythm discussed in Chapter 8. Again, any decent guitarist or piano player can look at this and show you how it's played.

Alternative Form of Basic Rock Rhythm Pattern

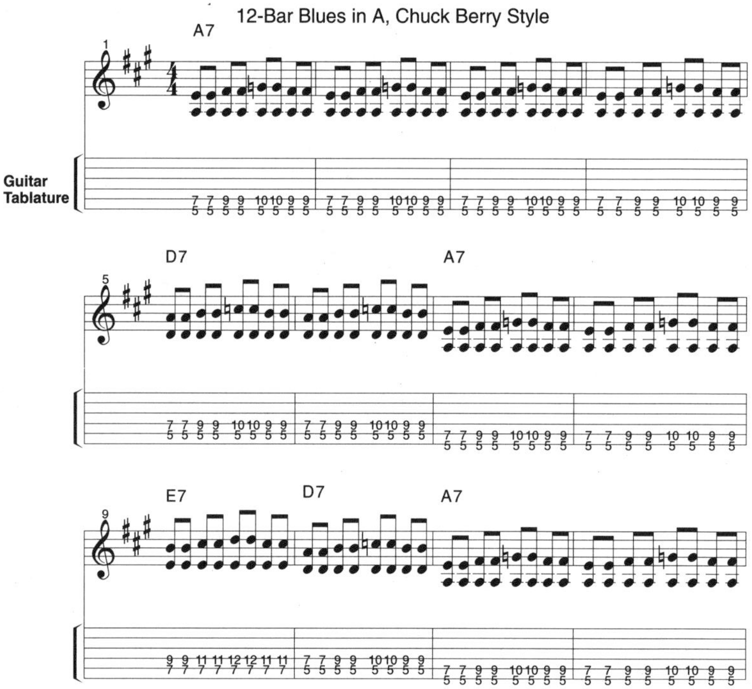

5

APPENDIX

Blues Scales in All Keys

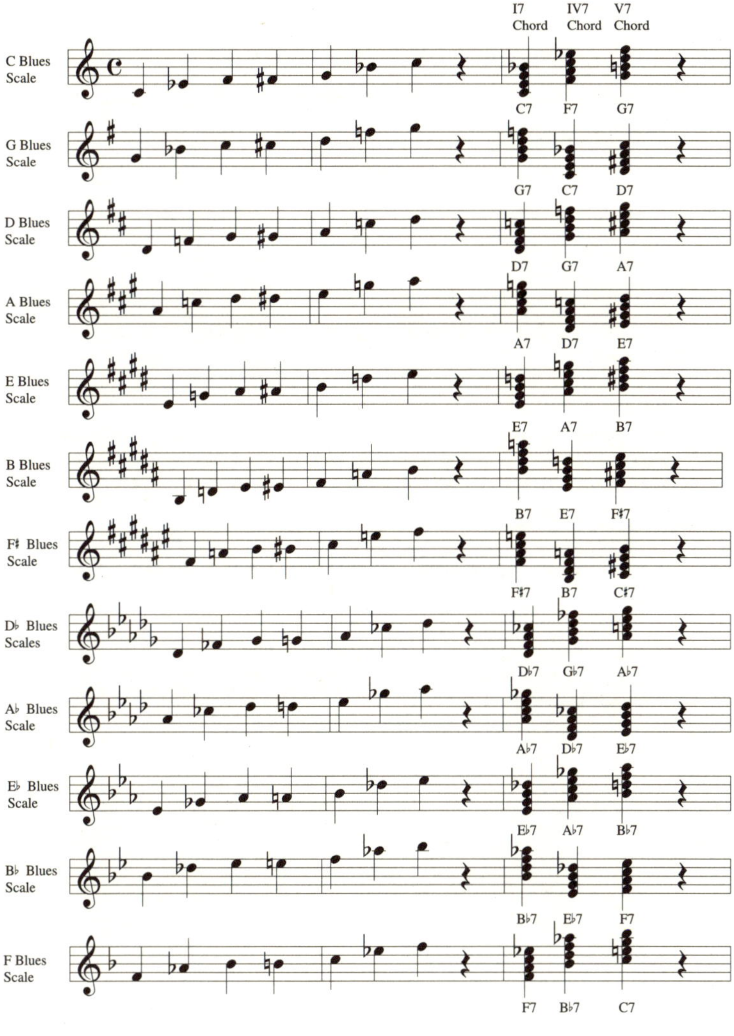

6

APPENDIX

Basic Shuffle Rhythm Pattern (In C for Piano)

The music below shows the basic shuffle rhythm pattern in the key of C, which is the first key for beginning piano. Any decent piano player can look at this and show you how to play this rhythm. (Since we haven't talked about the bass clef, we've written it in the treble clef, which is a little high for a left-hand rhythm. Once you get the hang of it, you'll want to move it an octave down the keyboard.)

Basic Shuffle Rhythm Pattern

12-Bar Blues in C

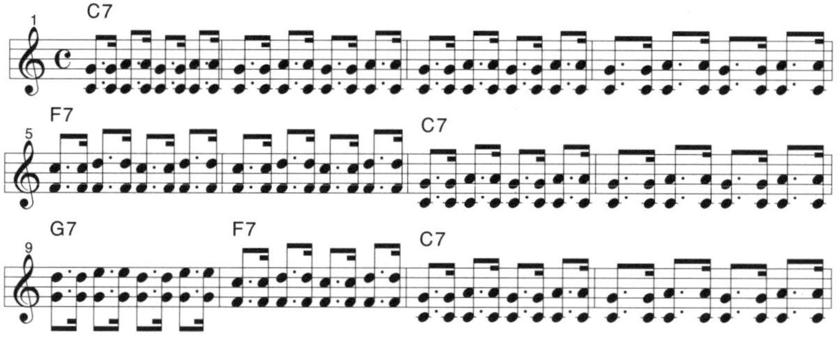

7

APPENDIX

Basic Rock Rhythm Pattern (In G for Piano)

The music below shows the basic rock rhythm pattern in the key of G. The pairing of the eighth notes in a ta ta, ta ta, ta ta rhythm is what gives it the rock feel. (As in the key of C, we've written this rhythm on the treble staff because we didn't want to get into explaining about the bass clef and staff. Your left hand will want to play the rhythm pattern a couple of octaves lower than written.)

Basic Rock Rhythm Pattern

12-Bar Blues in G, Chuck Berry Style

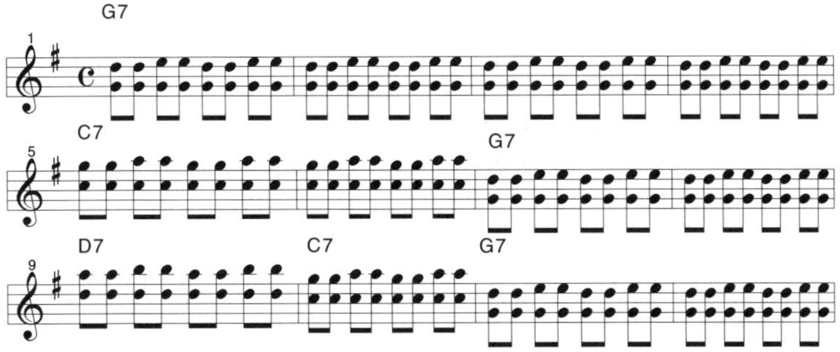

HOW THIS METHOD CAME ABOUT

Bob Ratcliff conceived this learning method while studying German composer Carl Orff's methods for teaching music to children under Avon Gillespie at the University of North Texas. Orff developed his now widespread method for teaching music to children by showing them how to improvise on the harmonies and rhythms of their native folk music, using a few notes from the pentatonic scale upon which much Western folk music is based.

Bob reasoned that if Orff could quickly draw small children into making improvised music using folk forms and the pentatonic scale, then Bob could do the same with teen-agers and adults using the blues form and the blues scale. Orff's approach provided Bob a framework to systematize the way he had learned to play jazz in junior high school – by using the blues scale to improvise over blues and jazz chord progressions.

He tested the idea on band students while student-teaching in Dallas, Texas, high schools. It worked. Since then, he has employed it with success in private lessons for adults and young adults in Dallas, Boise and Pullman, Wash., where he is completing his master of arts degree in music at Washington State University.